Handmade Books and Albums

An Introduction to Creative Bookbinding

Marie Ryst

Translation by Josh Heuman
Illustrations by Christian Lefebvre
Photographs by Jeanbor

Design Books

D1556255

To Catherine
To Christian, our children,
and our grandchildren

ACKNOWLEDGMENTS
The author thanks Melody Perherin, for permission
to show her leaf album (page 78), made in bookbinding class;
Roger and Andrée Lefebvre, Morgane Gallois and Thierry Wintz,
and all her students, young and old.
The publisher thanks Monique Lallier, for technical help
with the translation.

English translation by Josh Heuman
Copyright © 1999 by Design Books

Originally published in French as:
Carnets ets albums
Marie Ryst
Copyright © Bordas Dessain et Tolra 1996

Composition and production by Ken Gross

Library of Congress Cataloging-in-Publication Data
Ryst, Marie.
    [Carnets et albums. English]
    Handmade books and albums: an introduction to creative bookbinding / Marie
Ryst; translation by Josh Heuman; illustrations by Christian Lefebvre; photographs
by Jeanbor.
        p.   cm.
    ISBN 1-55821-570-0
    1. Bookbinding. 2. Notebooks—Design. 3. Albums—Design. I. Title.
    Z271.R97 1999
    686.3—dc21   98-44072
                                                                      CIP

Published by Design Books
Design Books are distributed by
The Lyons Press
123 West 18th Street
New York NY 10011
5   4   3   2   1
Printed in Italy

Preface

Writing, drawing, sketching, painting, collecting ... each of these activities is not only a form of expression, but also provides some of the myriad reasons for making handmade artists' books and albums, whether for yourself or to give as gifts. Whether you are searching for a special book in which to save your precious photographs, want to recover an old favorite whose cover is damaged, or make a boring store-bought item into an object of art, you can transform any book through the art of bookmaking. There is no limit to what you can do. In these pages you will learn about books and how they are made as well as styles and techniques from around the world for their production. So, let your imagination run wild, learn to express your creativity through this ancient yet contemporary art, and be initiated into the techniques of bookbinding.

Contents

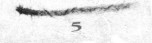

The writing surface

The history of written communication stretches back 20,000 years. It begins with drawings and paintings such as those in the Lascaux caves. Much later, signs and symbols developed. These were imprinted on tablets of soft clay with sharpened reeds; incised on stone, metal, or wax-covered wood or ivory tablets; traced on fragments of bone or bamboo; or painted on silk . . .

Later still, the Egyptians would use a new material: papyrus, the older cousin of paper, from which the younger relative takes its name. Papyrus is a kind of reed that grows abundantly in the Nile River valley. After removing the skin from its fibrous stalk, the ancient Egyptians cut its pith into thin strips; these were laid on a flat stone in successive layers—one horizontal, one vertical. They then hammered the assembled strips and, after drying and polishing them with a stone, glued many pieces together to make a roll of papyrus several yards (meters) long.

Around 200 B.C., King Eumenius of Pergamon, in Asia Minor, discovered a process for producing parchment. The essential material (most often sheepskin) was shaved, scraped, degreased in a lime bath, dried, rubbed with chalk, and finally polished with pumice stone. The very smooth parchment that resulted would be used as the writing surface for illuminated manuscripts.

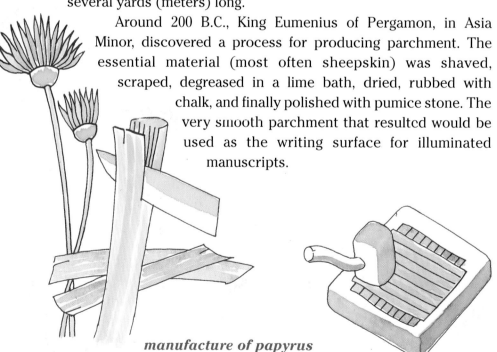

manufacture of papyrus

and books

The book

FROM SCROLL TO CODEX: THE BIRTH OF THE BOOK. Initially, papyrus, parchment, and silk manuscripts were rolled around painted wood or ivory rods with sculpted ends, called *umbelici.* Sometimes the scroll was enclosed in a hollow wood or metal cylinder. Later, the pages were folded in an accordion pattern, and placed between two pieces of wood that were held together with a band. The next step was to slit the folds on the right side, sew the left-hand folds, and write on both sides of the paper. Thus the Greco-Roman *codex,* named for its square shape, was born. Codexes were protected by an extra sheet of parchment, which acted as a cover.

THE ORIGIN OF PAPER. Although it takes its name from the Egyptian papyrus, paper as we know it first appeared in China in the second century B.C. Although earlier writing materials have not survived, there is evidence of experimentation with these materials, and fibrous scraps probably gave rise to the modern form. Paper traveled to the West by the trade routes and reached Europe in the twelfth century by way of the Moors. First Spain and then Italy began to make paper. Around the middle of the fourteenth century, the French learned the art of making paper from the Italians, and built the first paper mills.

FROM FIBER TO PAPER. The essential part of the paper mill is the pulp vat. In the first mills, linen, hemp, or cotton was first sorted and cut, before being "distressed," cut once more, and then pounded with mallets. The pounding separated and thinned the cellulose fibers of the material. The resulting pulp was then drained, whitened, and mixed with size; the size gave the paper a degree of impermeability. The product was then mixed in the pulp vat and warmed to a constant, medium temperature. To make the sheets of paper, a screen was dipped into the vat, coming out covered with pulp, and left to drain. The moist fibers were pressed on felt, hung to dry, sorted, smoothed, beaten, pressed again under weights, counted into 500-sheet reams, pressed for a night, and finally packaged for sale.

The Dutch paper mill, with its rotating cylinder fitted with lathes to replace mallets, perfected the process of paper manufacture. The Englishman Brian Donkin built the first machine to produce dry sheets. This innovation automated all phases of the papermaking process, from the removal of the pulp from the vats to the drying of the paper. Finally, in the mid-nineteenth century, as the supply of fabric materials dwindled, wood was added to the pulp. Today's papers are 95 percent wood.

FROM PAPER TO THE BOUND BOOK. Printing presses used large sheets of paper. These sheets were folded into sections assembled according to "signatures," the small numbers located on the bottom right-hand side of the first page of each section. Sewn together by hand or with a sewing machine, the assembled sections formed a book block. The spine was covered with glue and the book block was inserted within a soft cover. The book block was then ready to be sent to the bookbinder.

The origins of bookbinding

Bookbinding developed to protect books from the ravages of time and, like books, it has evolved over the centuries. Until the twelfth century, it was the province of the monasteries. Monks who were "the binders of books" sewed manuscripts, richly illuminated by rubricators, using leather thongs made from cows' tendons that formed raised bands on the spine. The ends of the leather thongs were inserted in notches carved in two thick pieces of wood—boards that served as the covers of the book. Eventually the leather thongs were replaced by hide, rolled parchment, and then thick hemp twine. The boards were sometimes covered with thick leather or cloth, and some were decorated with pieces of ivory, gilded copper set with jewels, gold, or silver. They were sometimes also ornamented with ornate clasps.

With the establishment of the Sorbonne, the French university, in 1257, and the consequent demand for books, a body of book-making artisans appeared. The first bookbinders (most often also booksellers) practiced their craft in Paris. By then, lighter and smaller books were covered in gold-embroidered or flower-patterned covers. Nonetheless, the traditional, religious work continued to be done, and the richly illustrated books of hours, perhaps the most famous illuminated manuscripts, were produced in the fifteenth century.

Gutenberg's invention of the printing press, between 1435 and 1440, popularized the book and in 1476 William Caxton set up as a printer and bookbinder in London. By the Renaissance, there were many bookselling and bookbinding studios in Europe. Wooden boards gave way to cardboard boards covered in leather, which were sometimes magnificently gilded. Marbled paper endpapers first appeared in 1634.

After the period of the French Revolution (a relatively low point in the art of bookbinding, and one in which many earlier books were destroyed), nineteenth-century bookbinders rediscovered and appropriated previous styles and techniques of gilding. The century was also one of great progress for industrial bookbinding, bequeathing a well-developed art to our own time, in which bookbinding has reached technical perfection.

Adhesives

PASTE. You can make paste from wheat, corn, or rice; most often, wheat flour is used. Paste is inexpensive, and can be used for all binding and covering projects. It dries more slowly than vinyl adhesives, allowing repair of errors and imperfections. Its best quality is its reversibility: you can easily separate two pieces that have been pasted together.

• ***Recipe for wheat-flour paste.*** Place a heaping tablespoon of wheat flour into a small pot. Little by little, add 1 cup (25cl) of water, stirring continually with a whisk or a wooden spoon, to make a mixture without lumps. Bring the mixture to a boil over medium heat and let simmer for two to three minutes, continuing to stir.

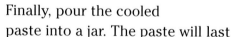

Remove the pot from the heat and plunge it into a basin of cold water, continuing to stir until the paste cools. Finally, pour the cooled paste into a jar. The paste will last for a while if refrigerated in a covered jar.

Water-soluble anti-mold pastes, with special chemical additives, are also available at bookbinding supply stores, sold as PVA.

materials

WATER PASTE. This adhesive is used for decorations in mosaic patterns of leather, called onlays. It consists of one teaspoon of fresh paste added to one-third cup (10cl) water.

POLYVINYL GLUE (PVA). Vinyl or plastic glue is a water-soluble white glue that can be diluted with water. (Careful: it stains!) It dries quickly, and thus demands a measure of skill. Unlike paste, it is irreversible, and you should avoid using it in direct contact with the pages of your books.

Papers

In earlier times, artisans could only make paper in a limited number of sizes. These papers sometimes bore the watermark of the maker, most often a design made with a brass wire placed on the paper mold, visible in the paper when it dried.

watermark for "raisin" format paper

Watermarks are the origin of our contemporary paper formats—the old names are still used to designate the modern formats.

There are two kinds of paper: laid paper and wove paper. Before the eighteenth century, all paper was laid paper, identifiable by the fine longitudinal lines and wider and more widely spaced transverse lines visible in the paper. Wove paper, in contrast, has a uniform surface; originally, it was supposed to resemble the skin of stillborn calf, which had been used for manuscripts since the thirteenth century for its smoothness and perfect whiteness. Wove and laid papers have ragged edges on all four sides. Machine-made papers produced from cotton and recycled papers can be used on both sides, are of good quality, and are much less expensive than fine, handmade, watermarked papers. Choose paper for your books according to the intended use: writing, calligraphy, drawing, gouache, watercolor, collage. Consider the structure of a paper's fibers and its resulting character; your project might call for a paper that is delicate or durable, transparent or opaque, thin or bulky, soft or tough.

For colored endpapers, you can buy Japanese papers with visible natural fibers, Indian papers to which certain plants and textiles have been added in manufacture, or marbled papers (either marbled in manufacture or afterward). You can decorate covers with natural or colored papers, which you can fold, crumple, tear, cut, overlay, weave, emboss, paint, wax. You should use paper that is strong, flexible, and easily sanded for lining the spine.

Paper comes in different weights, measured in pounds per 500-sheet ream or, in the metric system widely used today, grams per square meter (gsm). Thin papers are lighter; thick papers are heavier. The name of a paper used to indicate its size: among the sheets made were foolscap, royal, crown, imperial, double elephant, raisin, eagle, and other evocative names. Although handmade paper is still available today under traditional names, commercially manufactured paper is now yielding to international standards.

In order to determine the number of unfolded sheets you will need, calculate the number and size of sheets yielded by folding a particular dimension of paper:

- folded in two (folio): one fold, two leaves, one one-sheet signature
- folded in four (quarto): two folds, four leaves, two one-sheet signatures
- folded in eight (octavo): three folds, eight leaves, four one-sheet signatures
- folded in sixteen (16mo): four folds, sixteen leaves, eight one-sheet signatures
- folded in thirty-two (32mo): five folds, thirty-two leaves, sixteen one-sheet signatures

  The sizes given are those of the signature before it is trimmed (see A glossary for bookbinding).

Cardboard and card stock

To make hard covers for your books, use gray card at least $\frac{1}{16}$ inch (2mm) thick, or thicker board if the size of the book calls for it. Cardboard is available from binding supply stores in different thicknesses from $\frac{1}{16}$ to $\frac{1}{8}$ inch (1.5–1mm). For soft covers use smooth manila card less than $\frac{1}{32}$ inch (0.2-0.1mm) thick, bristol board, colored mat board, card, or tan corrugated cardboard (which can be painted in your choice of color).

Thread and cord

Linen thread is lightly waxed and sold in spools; it is available in different thicknesses. Hemp twine is made from two strands twisted together, specially prepared for bookbinding.

Fabrics

The muslin or calico used to strengthen the spine of a book can be replaced by a piece of lightweight linen.

1. Steel ruler
2. Mechanical pencil
3. Foam roller
4. Steel square with foot
5. Zinc or PVC cutting board
6. Bookbinding scissors
7. Hammer
8. 6-inch (15cm) bone folder
9. Craft knife
10. Flat square
11. Dividers (with screw adjustment for quick extension)
12 and 13. Paste brushes for applying adhesives
14. PVA glue
15. Fine- and medium-grit sandpaper

16. Heavy ruler for cutting
17. Wooden boards, 8 x 12in (20 x 30cm) and 12 x 16in (30 x 40cm)
18. Awl
19. Bookbinder's steel cutter
20. Weights
21. Glazier's clips
22. Two round punches nos. 5 and 6
23. Striking block
24. Tweezers
25. Heavy-duty utility knife or cutter
26. Flat-tipped chisel for tapes

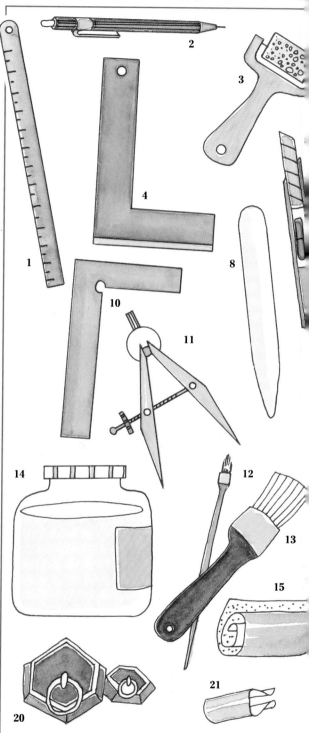

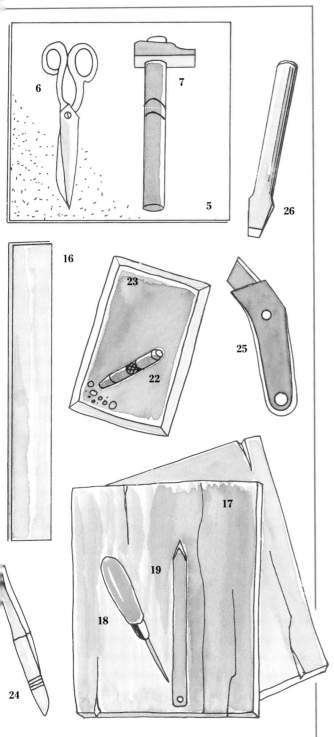

Other tools and materials useful for making books

- a resin folder
- a steel-bladed knife for tearing paper
- a light-colored grease (wax) pencil for making guide marks on dark paper
- a metal tapemeasure, 1 yard (1m) long
- drawing (bulldog) clips
- a small brush
- blunt-tipped sewing needles; thumbtacks or pushpins, to attach tapes to the sewing frame
- transparent double-sided tape
- a small metal saw for sawing signatures
- two pieces of card
- two sheets of lightweight plastic, such as mylar
- one right triangle for squaring picture windows
- a scalpel with a #10 blade for mosaic decoration (the scalpel can also serve as a general cutting tool), and a small agate burnisher, to polish the sanded edges of your books
- finally, a soft cloth to cover and protect unfinished works

a glossary . . .

Agate. A very hard stone mounted on a burnishing tool, used to polish a book's edges.

Bevel. To cut the edge of a piece of leather, card stock, or cardboard at an angle.

Board. A thick piece of wood or cardboard used to press books.

Book block. All the signatures of a book sewn together.

Bookbinder's press. A combination press, consisting of two kinds of vise, for pressing paper, and for fitting spines.

Case. The boards within which the book block is encased, glued to the endpapers.

Chemise. A decorative wrapper that protects a book before it is put in a slipcase.

Doublure. The inside of a cover board.

Cover boards. Pieces of cardboard cut to size for covers.

Covering. The operation of applying a decorative cover to the cover boards and spine.

Edge. Any of the three sides of the book.

Endpaper. A folio of paper placed at the beginning or end of a book for protection (white endpaper) or decoration (colored endpaper).

Folio. Two pages of a book, comprising a recto and a verso page.

Fore-edge. The side of the book opposite the spine.

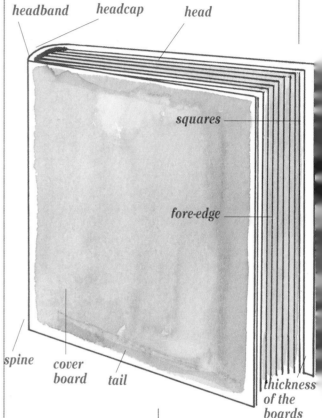

headband   *headcap*   *head*

squares

fore-edge

spine   *cover board*   *tail*   *thickness of the boards*

Head. The top of the book.

Headband. A hand-stitched protection and decoration for the spine at the head and tail of a book.

Headcap. The curved pieces of leather inserted at both ends of the spine to protect the headbands.

Jaspering. The operation of applying color to the three sides of a book with a brush and a screen.

for bookbinding

Newsprint. Absorbent waste paper used to protect the work surface when gluing.

Onlay. A technique of applying other leathers to a cover.

Paring. The operation of thinning leather by hand or with a paring machine.

Recto. The right-hand page of a book, as opposed to the verso, or left-hand page.

Shoulders. The protruding parts on the sides of the spine, fashioned to house the cover boards.

Skin. The outside of a piece of hide, opposite the flesh side.

Spine. The sewn or glued side of a book, opposite the fore-edge.

Squares. The part of the cover boards that extends past the pages of the book.

Tail. The bottom of the book.

Tapping. Aligning the pages of a book by stacking the pages and dropping the sides against a hard surface, turning the stack a quarter-turn each time.

Trim. To make a clean cut along the entire edge of a piece of paper or cardboard.

Trimming. The operation of cutting the edges of a book to straighten them and make them a uniform size.

Turn-ins. The extra margin of covering material extending beyond the cover board that is folded over and glued to the reverse of the board.

Verso. The left-hand page of a book, as opposed to the recto, or right-hand page.

Witness. The smallest in a set of folded sheets, used to determine the final size of the trimmed sheets. The witness sheet is left untrimmed and has irregular edges.

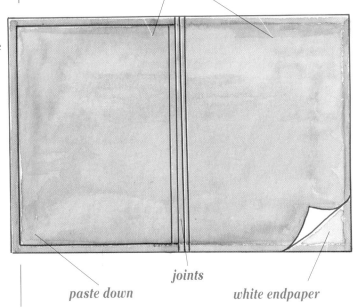

colored flyleaves

paste down

joints

white endpaper

The grain of paper

Commercial papers are produced in a roll, which is run off cylinders. With the speed at which these rollers spin, the paper fibers tend to align in the direction of their movement. The paper folds more easily "with the grain," along the axis of manufacture, than "across the grain." When exposed to moisture, the fibers expand more in width than in length; when the water evaporates and the paper dries, the fibers and the papers contract along the axis of elongation, against the grain, perpendicular to the axis of manufacture.

Grain direction determines how the paper will behave when folded or glued. If the grain of a book's pages runs the wrong way, the pages will curl with humidity; a board covered with paper on only one side will warp as its fibers contract, even after pressing. When covering boards, you must take this elongation into account, and reduce one of the dimensions of the covering paper accordingly.

There are several ways to determine the direction of a paper's grain. You can roll the sheet along both axes: resistance will be less, and the curve will be smoother, with the grain. You can also wet a small square of the paper: it will arch against the grain, along the axis of elongation (some papers, however, resist moisture, and are called "inert"). If the paper is thin, you can pull its edges between the nails of your thumb and forefinger; the side that curls most follows the axis of elongation. Finally, paper tears more easily with than across the grain. The grain must always run parallel to the spine of the book.

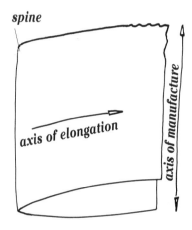

spine

axis of elongation

axis of manufacture

techniques

Folding and cutting paper

Books and albums consist of several folios. Each folio consists of two leaves, joined at the spine. Each leaf, in turn, is made up of two pages: a recto (the front side) and a verso (the back side). A single sheet folded once (folio) yields a signature of two leaves and four pages. The blank books described here are made of unfolded sheets or from signatures of large sheets of paper that must be folded and cut.

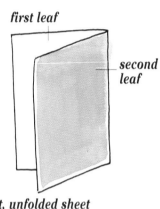

first leaf

second leaf

Lay the sheet down flat, with the longer side facing you.

First fold: the folio

Hold the lower-left corner of the sheet in place with your left hand.

flat, unfolded sheet

With your right hand, bring the lower-right corner exactly over the lower-left corner. Adjust the placement with your left thumb and index finger. The two shorter sides of the sheet must line up exactly.

With the tip of the folder, crease the fold, moving from center to each edge.

first fold

Turn the folded sheet 90 degrees clockwise. Slide the folded sheet to the edge of your work surface. Hold it flat in place with your left hand. Cut the fold with a sharp steel-bladed knife, to yield two leaves.

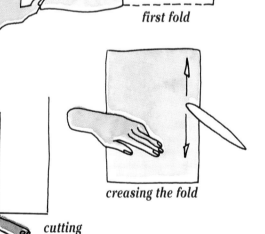

creasing the fold

cutting the fold

the basic techniques

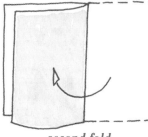

second fold

Second fold: quarto

Fold and cut these two leaves in the same way, giving four leaves.

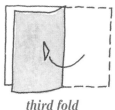

third fold

Third fold: octavo

Fold and cut these four to make eight leaves.

You can fold the paper again to obtain sixteen leaves, and again for thirty-two; stop when you reach the desired size. If you leave the last fold uncut, the resulting signatures can be sewn.

Cutting

Whether you cut an entire edge with a scalpel, a knife, or a cutter, you must make a straight, clean cut.

To determine a cutting line, make light guide marks with a pencil or the point of your cutting tool at the top and bottom of the sheet. It's best to cut while standing.

Place the sheet on a zinc sheet or cutting mat, with the cutting line at a right angle to the edge of the work surface. Position the heavy ruler to protect the part of the sheet you want to keep—cut on the "outside." Put the cutting tool on the guide mark that is closer to you, and move the ruler so that the base touches the blade. Move the cutting tool to the farther guide mark, and pivot the ruler against the blade with the thumb and index finger of your left hand

determining the cutting line

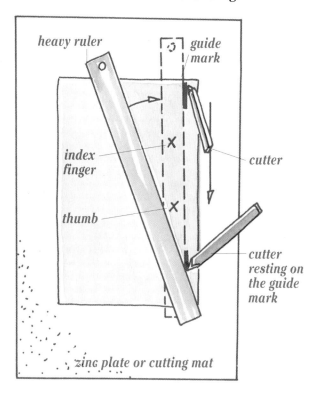

heavy ruler — guide mark — index finger — thumb — cutter — cutter resting on the guide mark — zinc plate or cutting mat (these should be spread apart along the ruler). Hold your thumb and finger firmly over the guide marks so that the ruler does not move. Hold the knife at a 45-degree angle, cutting with the tip of the blade rather than the diagonal edge. Cut toward yourself, first with a light pass to score the paper (thus avoiding tearing or crimping it), and then make several more passes until the paper or cardboard comes apart of its own accord. Change knife blades often.

Cutting a perfect rectangle with square and cutter

This operation yields a perfect rectangle, with four 90-degree corners.

Start with a piece of cardboard or paper that is a little larger than the desired dimensions. Place the heavy ruler along one long side of the rectangle. Carefully slide the square along the ruler. Make two guide marks along the square, and cut along the length of the ruler (see page 20).

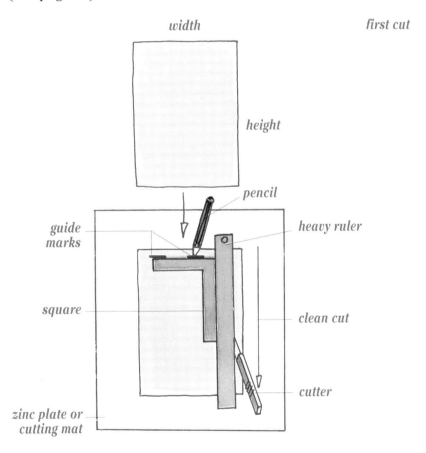

width   first cut

height

pencil

guide marks

heavy ruler

square

clean cut

cutter

zinc plate or cutting mat

techniques

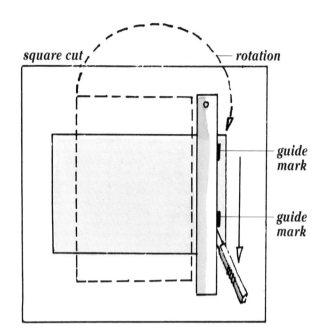

square cut   *rotation*

guide mark

guide mark

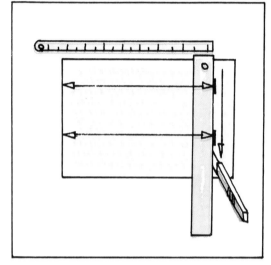

cut to the final height

Turn the paper 90 degrees and, with the square perpendicular to the first cut, make a second cut. Then, along a line perpendicular to this second cut, make two guide marks to determine the final height of the cut sheet. It is best to use the metal ruler here. Place the heavy ruler along the guide marks, and cut. Turn the sheet another 90 degrees, make two guide marks to indicate the final width of the cut sheet, and cut. With the square, check that the four corners are right angles.

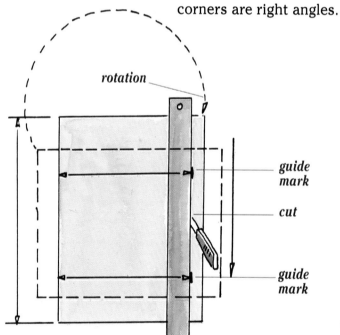

rotation

guide mark

cut

guide mark

cut to the final width

Gluing

To glue a piece of paper, first place it in the middle of a piece of waste paper (newsprint) larger than the piece to be glued. Hold the paper in your left hand and apply glue from the center to the outside in a "bicycle-spoke" pattern, applying glue right over onto the waste paper. Leave the brush resting on the paper while you change the position of your fingers on the page, then fill in the "spokes" of the glue, spreading it uniformly, without spots of over-application. To keep the paper from curling, pull the waste paper over the edge of the work surface, while supporting the work with your left hand. Quickly jerk the waste paper from underneath the sheet, catching the far side of the glued sheet so that it does not curl up. Place the sheet on the support. With the flat of your hand, smooth the paper from the center to the edges, pushing air bubbles to the outside. If what you are gluing is fragile, put a sheet of thin paper over it for protection before affixing the work to the support.

Glued work should always dry under weights, between two boards. Some work is best pressed in a press for a few minutes (still between the boards) before being left to dry under weights. It is very important to allow enough drying time.

To avoid glue stains on other parts of the book, slide a sheet of plastic under the glued parts while the work dries under weights.

Throughout this book, these gluing operations are referred to thus: Press for a few minutes, and then let dry thoroughly under weights.

glued

books

*A collection
of words,
simple and
refined,
just for
you alone, for
times
of reflection
and
leisure . . .*

Preparation

THE MATERIALS. Sheets of paper (the size and number depend on the desired size and page count of your book); PVA; fine muslin; corrugated cardboard, or bristol board, for cover boards; paper or fabric for covering; elements for closure and decoration; linen thread and paper, fabric, or leather, for headbands; plastic sheets, newsprint or waste paper, and card to protect your work.

THE MODEL. Make a model for your project to allow you to see your concept in concrete form, and to help you plan how to produce it. Such a model allows you to check whether the project is technically feasible and to establish harmony and balance.

Note: Glued books are not as strong as sewn books, so a glued book should not be too thick or too large. The pages can be simple sheets or folios.

Construction

THE PAGES. Fold and cut (with a steel-bladed knife or a board cutter) sheets of paper to make the desired size and number of pages (see page 19). Stack the pages and align them perfectly by dropping the spine and tail sides against a hard surface several times, turning the stack a quarter-turn each time. (This operation is called "tapping.")

TRIMMING THE LEAVES. It is nearly impossible to fold paper so that it is exactly square, and the top and bottom sides will not all be the same height. To correct the disparities, you must trim the leaves. This technique of cutting leaves one by one is similar to cutting with a board cutter in binding. Tap the stack on the tail and hold it in one

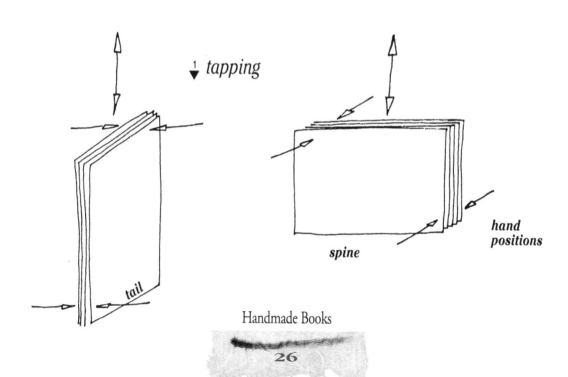

tapping

spine

hand positions

tail

Handmade Books

hand. Find the shortest leaf. Remove it from the stack and measure its height. Then tap the stack on the spine side. Find the narrowest leaf, remove it, and measure its width. Cut all the leaves a fraction of an inch (1mm) short of these measurements. (See "A glossary for bookbinding," page 17.)

APPLYING GLUE TO THE SPINE. Carefully place the stack on your work surface, with the spine protruding a little over the edge. Hold the stack in place with a weight and your hand. Then apply diluted PVA to the spine, keeping the brush at right angles to the spine and moving from top to bottom so that a little glue gets in between the leaves.

Tap the spine on the work surface to align the leaves. Remove any glue from the faces of the first and last sheets. Move the stack back to the work surface, the spine again a little over the edge. Check the alignment of the leaves once more and carefully square them off. Put a weight on the book block and let dry.

SAWING GLUED BOOKS. After gluing the leaves, make several transverse notches in the spine with a small metal saw; these notches will eventually help to hold the spine together securely (this is called sawing). The operation requires a press, which you can buy at

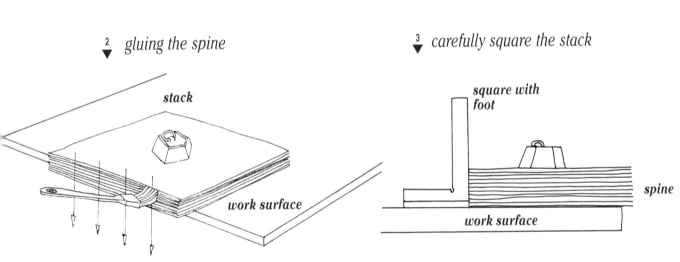

2 ▼ *gluing the spine*

stack

work surface

3 ▼ *carefully square the stack*

square with
foot

spine

work surface

glued books

specialty binding supply stores, or you can make one yourself following one of the models below. (To set the press and saw the spine, see "Sewn books with sunken cords," page 66.) Reglue the spine, then slip pieces of linen thread a little longer than the width of the spine into the notches. After the glue dries, cut the excess thread flush with the spine.

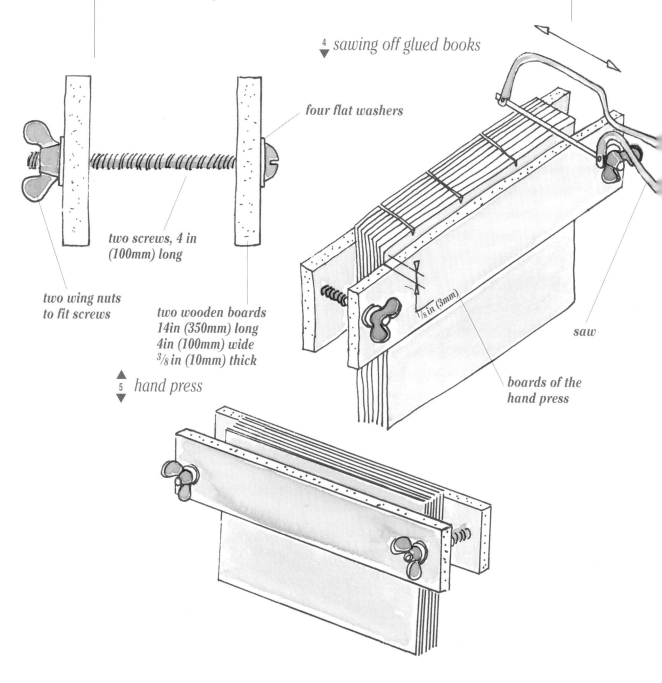

4 *sawing off glued books*

four flat washers

two screws, 4 in (100mm) long

two wing nuts to fit screws

two wooden boards 14in (350mm) long 4in (100mm) wide ³/₈ in (10mm) thick

1/8 in (3mm)

saw

boards of the hand press

5 *hand press*

APPLYING THE LINEN. Cut a small strip of linen (or other light fabric) of the same height as the book and 1½ in (4cm) wider than the spine. Apply another coat of PVA to the spine. Carefully center the fabric so that ¾ in (2cm) extends over each of the cover boards. Pull the linen taut and affix it to the spine with the flat part of a folder. Then glue the sides of the linen that extend over the first and last signatures, trimming to even if necessary.

THE HEADBANDS. You can make headbands with paper, fabric, or pared leather. Cut two small rectangles of the material, ¾ in (2cm) tall, and a little wider than the spine. The headbands are constructed around a piece of linen cord whose diameter is a little less than the squares. Apply PVA to the inside of the two rectangles and place the taut cords on top. Fold the rectangles over, then rub the cord well with the bone folder. Let dry for fifteen minutes. Apply glue to the head and tail ends of the spine, ¾ in (2cm) from the edges, and apply the bands. Slip them into place so that the raised part rests on the very edges of the book. Affix the bands to the spine and rub well with the bone folder; then let dry and trim the excess from the spine.

In the Middle Ages, strips of leather wrapped around linen cord were attached to the spine and inserted into the signatures. These "headbands" served to strengthen the binding. When books were covered in leather, the headbands also made it possible to keep the leather on the spine at the same height as that on the cover. Since the sixteenth century, headbands have been constructed from silk rolled around spills of rolled paper. They help protect the book, and also serve a decorative function.

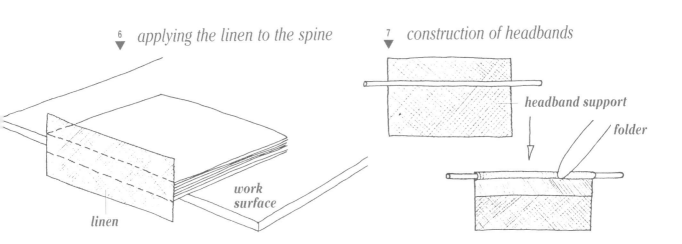

6 *applying the linen to the spine*

work surface

linen

7 *construction of headbands*

headband support

folder

glued books

THE COVER. Here, the cover is flexible, and made of a single piece of material. Measure to give a small square of ⅟₁₆ in (2mm) over the head, tail, and fore-edge. The total width of the cover is thus two squares plus twice the width of the signatures plus the width of the spine. The total height is two squares plus the height of the signatures.

The part of the cover that extends past the signatures is called the "square." Starting around the twelfth century, covers began to be cut larger than the pages, to protect them.

• ***Cutting the cover.*** Cut the material for the cover (see page 21), and mark the location of the squares and spine with the point of the dividers. Holding a ruler along the guide marks that determine where the spine should be folded, crease the edges of the spine by running the folder along the fold. If the cover is tough, you can cut halfway through the material. These operations aren't necessary for corrugated cardboard covers; for these simply sand the edges of the cover so that it will be neat.

• ***Covering the outside of the cover.*** The paper or fabric used for covering must be larger than the boards to be covered, by ⁹⁄₁₆ in (1.5cm) all around. You can use unfolded fabric, provided you glaze it first so that the glue does not seep through.

• ***Glazing the fabric.*** Apply PVA to a sheet of glass larger than the fabric. Place the fabric on the glass face up, carefully affixing it to the glass and remove; let dry. Repeat a second time before covering the book. The width of the material should equal the width of the cover plus the width of the two turn-ins on the inside of the cover. Its height should be the height of the cover plus the height of the two turn-ins. Cut the fabric or paper (see pages 20–21). Place

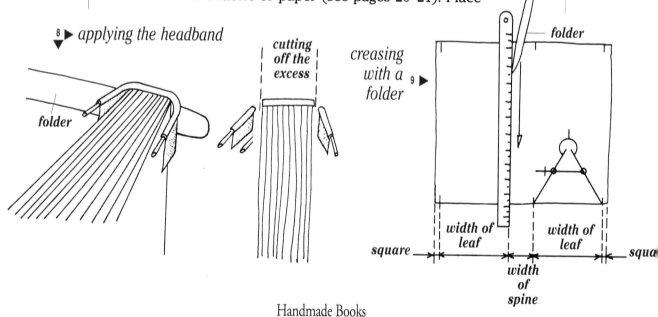

8 ▶ *applying the headband*

folder

cutting off the excess

creasing with a 9 ▶ *folder*

folder

width of leaf

square

width of spine

width of leaf

squa

Handmade Books

the cover face down on the covering material, leaving the proper squares all around. Make light pencil marks on the material to mark the edges of the cover at the four corners (these guide marks are necessary to ensure proper placement of the cover). Put the covering material face down on a clean piece of waste paper and carefully apply glue to the inside. Place the cover face down on the material, following the guide marks indicating the placement of the turn-ins. Lift up the whole stack, and place it on another, clean piece of waste paper, the covering material face up, its recto facing you. Holding your hands flat, softly smooth over the cover through a thin sheet of plastic (to avoid shiny marks on the cover from rubbing with the bone folder). Smooth from the middle to the edges, pushing any bubbles to the outside. Turn the work over, so that the cover

10 ▼ boards face up, and cut the corners of the covering material at a 45-degree angle, leaving at the corners an amount of fabric that is one and a half times the thickness of the board. Apply a light coat of glue to the longer edges of the excess material (running from the head to the tail of the board), remove the blotter, and move the board so that 11 ▼ the longer edges hang over the work surface a little. Then fold over the excess inside the cover board.

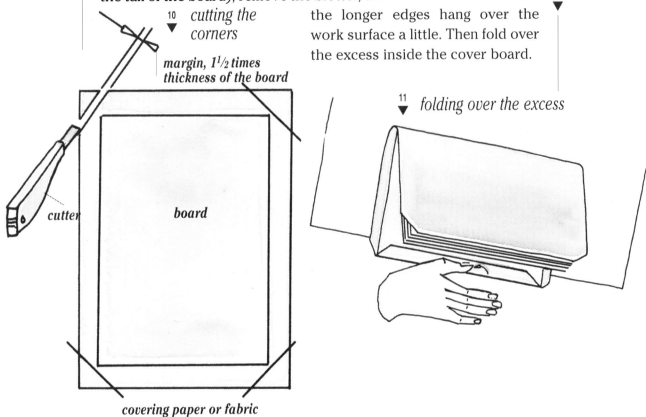

10 ▼ *cutting the corners*

margin, 1½ times thickness of the board

cutter

board

covering paper or fabric

11 ▼ *folding over the excess*

Start by folding at the middle; with your thumb on the lower edge of the cardboard, hold the covering material taut. Then, rotating your hand, affix the material first to the middle, and then to the top of the board with your fingers, applying enough pressure for proper adhesion. With the flat part of the folder softly smooth along the edge of the board and then the turn-in portion. Fold the second long side in the same way. With the folder, carefully fold over the small lobes formed at the two corners of each of the shorter sides. The corners should come to sharp right angles. Apply a light coat of glue to the shorter sides and fold them over. Put the signatures back inside the cover, and slide card or blotting paper between each covered board and the first and last pages, so that the moist glue does not seep onto the rest of the book while it dries under weights (see page 23). Now trim the turn-ins: with a compass, mark the four turn-ins ⁵⁄₁₆ in (8mm) away from the edge of the cover boards. Connect the compass guide marks with a ruler, and lightly trim away the excess covering material with a cutter or scalpel, without cutting the board (see page 20). Carefully remove the excess paper or fabric by lifting with a cutter, and lightly sand the inside of the cover.

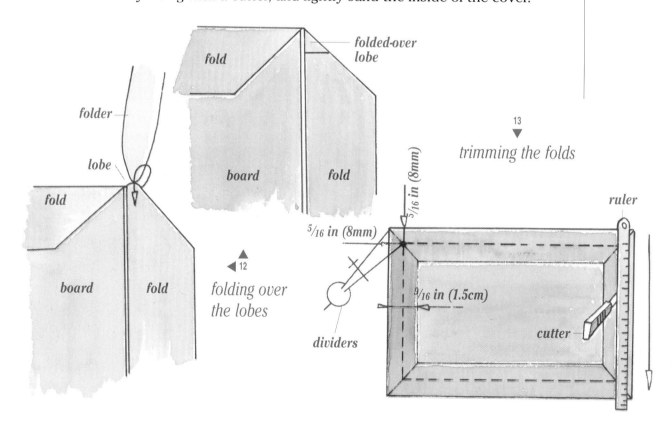

folder

lobe

fold

board

fold

folded-over lobe

fold

board

fold

▲ 12
folding over the lobes

dividers

⁵⁄₁₆ in (8mm)

⁵⁄₁₆ in (8mm)

⁹⁄₁₆ in (1.5cm)

13 ▼
trimming the folds

ruler

cutter

THE CLOSURE. To construct a closure on the cover of your book, first mark the placement of the band with light guide lines on the back cover. Make slits with the knife and thread the band through the slit, gluing ⅜ in (1cm) to the cover board. Lightly strike the cover with a hammer to flatten the part where the band goes. If you are using a hemp band, separate the fibers with an awl and glue to the inside of the cover board in a fan pattern. Or if you prefer, the fan can be part of the decoration— in that case, glue it after the casing of the book.

In the Middle Ages, monks enclosed manuscripts between two boards tied together with a strap, to protect the pages from warping. The strap was later replaced by thongs attached to the edges of wooden boards. Still later, metal buttons and hooks were used, and were called clasps.

14 ▼

15 ▼

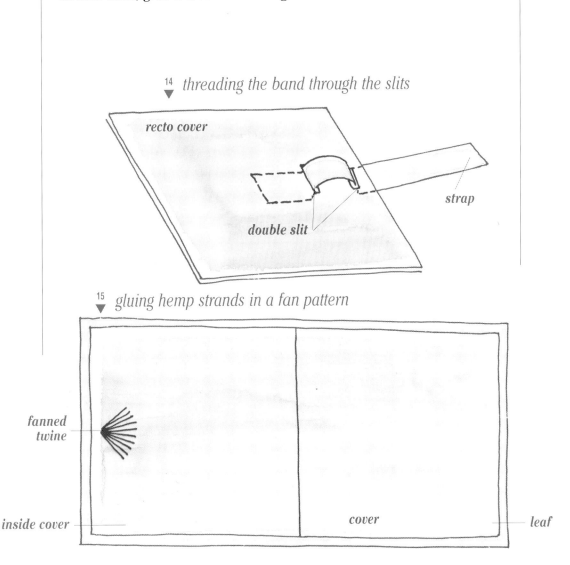

14 ▼ *threading the band through the slits*

recto cover

double slit

strap

15 ▼ *gluing hemp strands in a fan pattern*

fanned twine

inside cover

cover

leaf

glued books

pierced and

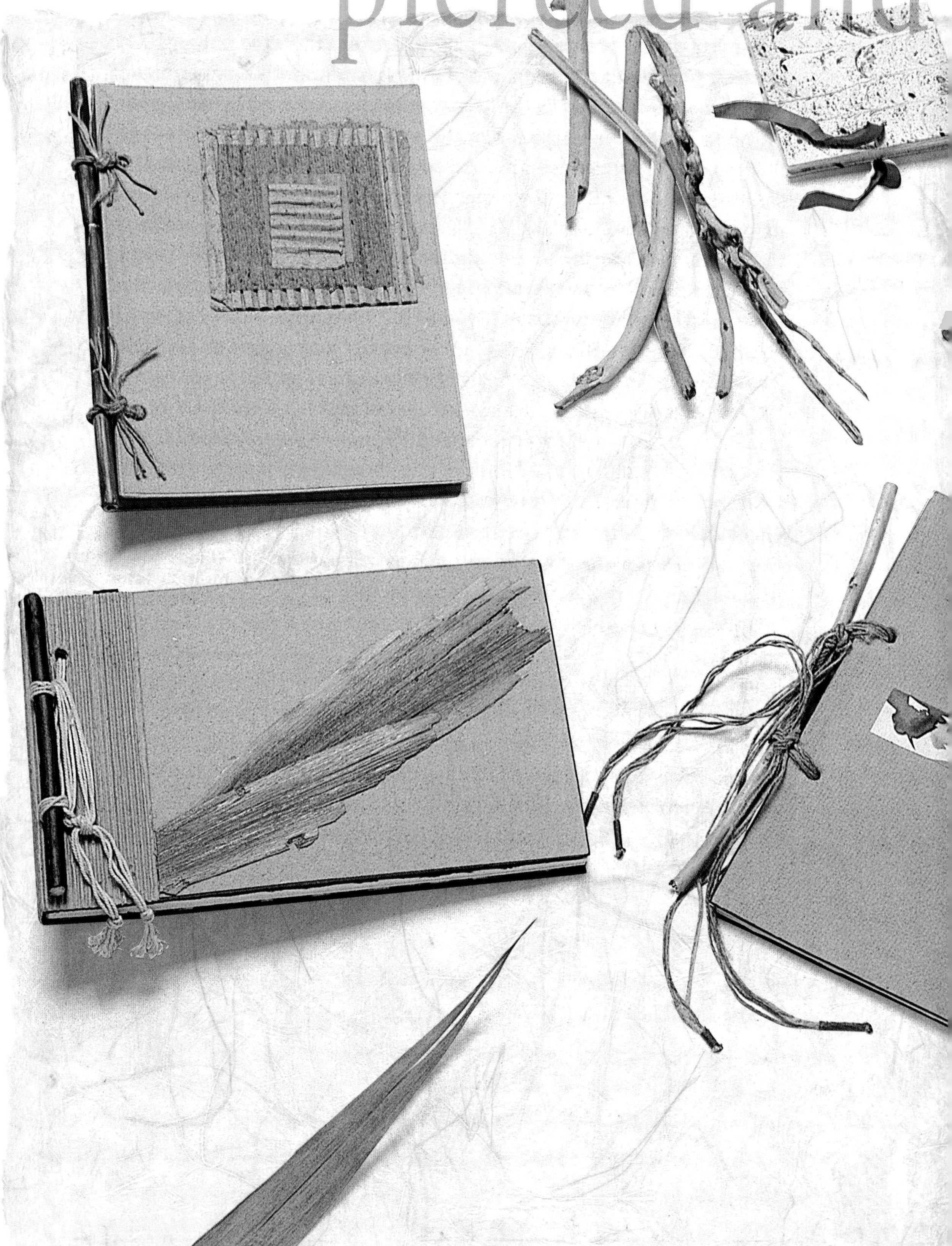

tied books

*Some pages
tied together
within a hard
cover, bits of
driftwood
and other
found objects,
and some
knotted
cords . . .*

Preparation

THE MATERIALS. Paper, for the pages of the book and its colored endpapers; gray cardboard 1/16 in (2mm) thick, for the cover boards; PVA; paper or fabric, for the cover; natural-toned linen thread; colored thread (optional); miscellaneous ornamental elements: a bamboo stalk, a piece of driftwood, or a branch—unfinished, sanded and waxed, or dyed with dilute acrylic ink (optional); plastic sheets, blotters, and card—to protect your work.

THE MODEL. For the book to open completely, the knots that bind it must be flexible. The sticks slipped through the string along the spine of these books have a decorative function, but also help to hold the books together when closed. The pages are simple unfolded sheets. Paper with irregular edges gives a nice decorative effect, reminiscent of pre-industrial paper manufacture. The spine side of the pages will be visible, and so must be as good-looking as the other sides. A variation on the pierced and tied book adds a decorative and functional hinge.

Construction

THE PAGES. Fold and cut sheets of paper for the pages of the book (see page 19). If the sheets have uneven edges, arrange the pages so that the edges that were not cut with a cutter are on the tail and fore-edge side of the book. Trim the head edge of the pages, following the same method as for glued books. Align and tap the sheets.

PRESSING THE PAGES. To flatten the sheets into a compact block, leave them under heavy pressure for twelve hours, or longer if possible.

paper press 1 ▼

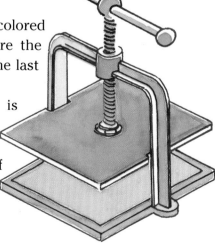

THE COLORED ENDPAPERS. Insert two sheets of colored paper for endpapers, before the first recto page and after the last verso page.

THE COVER. The cover is composed of two boards.

The first book presses were built like wine-presses. They were very difficult to close, and were replaced in the nineteenth century by percussion presses.

Measure to give only a very small square—about 1/32 in (1mm)—so that the head, tail, and fore-edge of the pages are a fraction within the cover boards. The width of the boards should be the width of the pages plus one square; the height should be the height of the pages plus two squares. Cut out two pieces of gray cardboard, a little larger than the desired dimensions of the cover, and then cut them down to the final measurements (see page 21). The cover boards must be exactly the same size and perfectly square. Sand the faces and edges of the boards smooth and clean.

• **_Covering the inside of the cover._** Covering the inner side of the cover of pierced and tied books, by folding the excess fabric over the recto of the cover, corresponds to the covering of the outside face of other books. (In bookbinding, you fold over the inner side.) First determine the dimensions of the paper or fabric, allowing for a ⅝ in (1.5cm) turn-in all around. The width should be two turn-ins plus the width of the board. The height should be two turn-ins plus the height of the board. Cut the material (see page 21), and position it face down on the work surface. Place the cover board on top, making sure the turn-ins are all equal. Lightly mark the location of the corners of the board on the covering material. Place the

In hand-bookbinding, decorative endpapers are most often made of marbled paper. Invented in Turkey, marbled paper first appeared in France in the seventeenth century; royal binder Macé Ruette first used it for endpapers in 1634. The colored endpaper was inserted between the inside cover and the first white endpaper to cover traces of glue and other imperfections. Endpapers, whether colored or white, protect the first pages of a work, in addition to serving a decorative function.

2 ▼ *cut out of gray cardboard . . .*

leaf   *cover board*   HEAD   *square*

SPINE

FORE-EDGE

square

width

TAIL

pierced and tied books

material face down on a clean piece of waste paper, apply glue, affix the cover board in proper position, and fold over the excess paper or fabric (turn-ins). Cover the other board in the same way. Let both dry under weights, and then trim the turn-ins down to $\frac{5}{16}$ in (8mm). (These operations are described in greater detail in the section on glued books.)

• **_Covering the outside of the cover._** First, determine the size of the paper or fabric required; then, cut the material $\frac{1}{16}$ in (2mm) smaller all around than the cover boards. If you are using paper, check its sensitivity to moisture before cutting it to final size (see page 18). The width and height will be those of the cover boards less twice $\frac{1}{16}$ in (2mm)—that is, $\frac{1}{8}$ in (4mm). Cut the material (see pages 20–21), check its fit, and correct the cut if necessary. Apply a light coat of glue and carefully affix the material to the outer face of the cover board, making sure the $\frac{3}{32}$ in (2mm) margin is even all around. Place a sheet of fabric on top of the covering material (so it does not stick to the boards of the press), press for a few minutes, and then let dry completely under weights after removing the plastic sheets.

ASSEMBLING THE BOOK. Clear your work surface of all the tools you have finished with, and arrange the material you will need to assemble the book. Place one of the cover boards face down on a sheet of paper. Tap the stack of pages until it is perfectly square, then carefully position it on the cover board, leaving the proper squares along the head, tail, and fore-edge. Place a square at the edge of the cover board.

Carefully place the other cover board face up on the stack, against the square; then move the square to each of the three other sides to align the cover boards. The pages of the book must not move during this operation, and the cover boards must be perfectly aligned. This delicate operation requires considerable care and precision; with several squares, it is easier to hold the

3 ▼

3 ▼ *assembly*

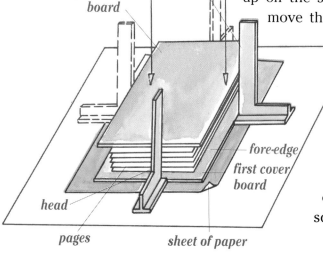

footed square

second cover board

fore-edge

first cover board

head

pages

sheet of paper

cover boards in place. Gently pull the base sheet of paper so that it hangs ¾ in (2cm) over the edge of the work surface. Check that the stack is still square, and then clamp the overhanging edge at both ends. Turn the stack and repeat for the remaining edges. If the covering material is fragile, slip small bands of cardboard or sturdy paper between the clamps and the cover board for protection. Determine where along the spine the two or three holes are to be made with the punch. These should not be too close to the head or tail. On the recto board, pencil an X at the center of the holes. Slide a piece of cardboard between the striking block and the book so that you do not ruin the cover (you can use a glued stack of heavy cardboard in place of the block). Balance the book on the block, and make up the difference in height between the striking block and the work surface by sliding a wooden block under the book, which at this point should be perfectly stable. Position the punch on one of the penciled Xs and drive it through the stack with a hammer. Remove the punch with a twisting motion. Make the remaining holes in the same fashion. Remove the clamps, and clean up the paper and cardboard around the holes with a pliers or hammer. To tie the book with linen thread, hang the spine over the edge of the work surface, holding the book in place with a weight. Cut a length of thread 12in (30cm) longer than four times the length of the book. Thread it through the holes following the illustration below.

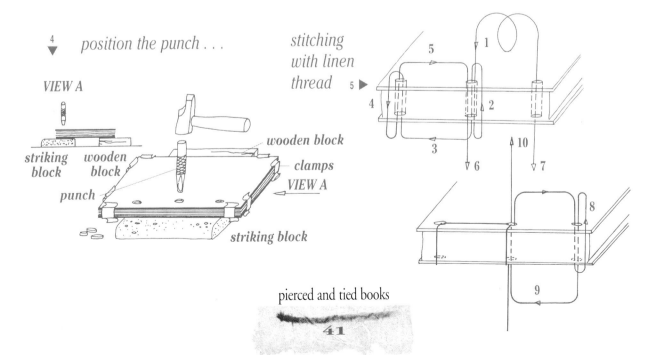

position the punch . . .

VIEW A

striking block

wooden block

punch

wooden block

clamps

VIEW A

striking block

stitching with linen thread

pierced and tied books

• **The "Seaside" notebook** (pages 36–37, center). For ease of manipulation, cut a fairly long piece of thread. Make a loop at one end, and hold it against the linen cord. Wrap the other end around the cord, coiling over the open part of the loop to close it. The loops should be very tight against one another. After the last loop, run the string through the ring, pull it taut to the other end of the cord, and cut away the excess. Repeat at both ends of all the cords, and apply any ornamental decoration with PVA glue. Slide the stick through the cords as shown below.

PIERCED AND TIED BOOK WITH "HINGE" (variation, page 36, lower left). The hinge on this "Italian-style" book (so called for the fact that width is greater than its height) makes it easier to open. It is constructed like other pierced and tied books, except for its recto (front) cover, described below.

• **The front cover.** A flexible hinge connects the two cover boards.
(1) The first front cover has a width of 1in (2.5cm). Its height is that of the pages plus two squares.
(2) The second front cover is the same width as the back cover, less 1in (2.5cm) for the first board and ³⁄₁₆ in (5mm) for the hinge. Its height is that of the pages plus two squares.
Cut and sand the cover boards.

• **Covering the inside of the covers.** First, determine the proper dimensions of the covering material. Its width must cover a ³⁄₈ in (1cm) turn-in plus the width of the first board (1) plus the ³⁄₁₆ in (5mm) space of the hinge plus the width of the second board (2) plus a second ³⁄₈ in (1cm) turn-in. Its height will equal one height of both

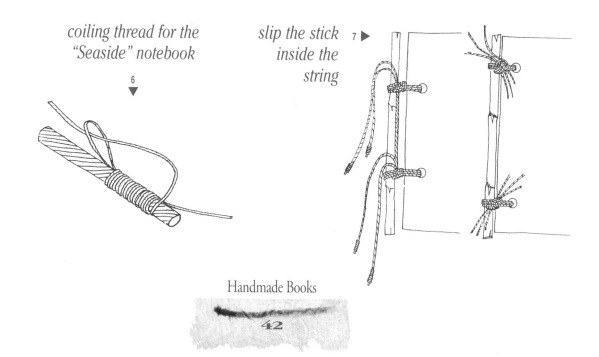

coiling thread for the
"Seaside" notebook

6 ▼

slip the stick 7 ▶
inside the
string

cover boards (1 and 2) plus two turn-ins. Cut the material, and place it face down on the work surface. Determine and mark the positions of the hinge and the squares. Lightly mark the four corners. Construct a template, ³⁄₁₆ in (5mm) wide, the same height as the cover, by gluing together several pieces of cardboard. Place the template along the space of the hinge before gluing the first front cover. Apply glue to all of the material and put the second board in place. Place the heavy ruler along the head fold; the ruler must be perfectly horizontal. Place the template in the space of the hinge and glue the second board. Fold over the extra material, and press for several minutes before letting dry under weights. Trim the turn-ins to ⁵⁄₁₆ in (8mm).

• ***Covering the outside of the covers.*** Check the sensitivity of your material to moisture (see page 18), and take its expansion into account when you calculate its final dimensions. The width should equal that of the first cover board plus twice the thickness of the cardboard plus ³⁄₁₆ in (5mm) for the hinge space plus the width of the second cover board less twice ¹⁄₁₆ in (2mm). The height will be that of the cover boards less twice ¹⁄₁₆ in (2mm). Check the material, and trim if necessary. Apply glue to the material, then position it on top of the cover boards, leaving the proper margin all around, affixing it to the boards with a folder pressed against the edges of the board next to the hinge. Press for several minutes, then let dry under weights.

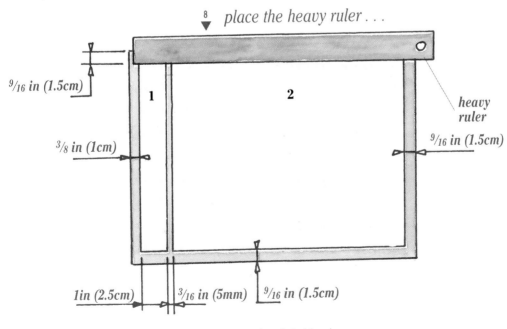

8 *place the heavy ruler . . .*

⁹⁄₁₆ in (1.5cm)

1

2

heavy ruler

⁹⁄₁₆ in (1.5cm)

³⁄₈ in (1cm)

1in (2.5cm) ³⁄₁₆ in (5mm) ⁹⁄₁₆ in (1.5cm)

pierced and tied books

accordion

books

*L*et your
vision
become
panoramic,
with
ancient
Chinese-
style
accordion
books.

Preparation

THE MATERIALS. Paper sold in rolls or in large widths for the pages of the book; PVA, wheat-flour paste, or wallpaper paste; $\frac{1}{16}$ in (2mm) gray cardboard and manila card for covers; paper for covering; ornamental elements and clasps (optional); sheets of plastic, waste paper, and card to protect your work.

THE MODEL. To reduce the number of tabs, it is best to use medium-weight (around 80-pound/120gsm) paper sold in wide widths, such a sheet measuring about 28¾ x 42 (75 x 105cm). If too thick, the paper will be difficult to fold; if too thin, it will lack stability. The picture window is a decorative device imported from framing. The front and back covers must be of the same thickness. You must glue the back board to a board of the same thickness as that which supports the image on the front board. The greatest difficulty in the construction of accordion books is the alignment of cover boards and pages for gluing. To make things easier, use wheat-flour paste or wallpaper paste—these adhesives, slower to dry than PVA, allow you to correct any potential errors.

Construction

THE PAGES. Determine the size of your sheets on the basis of the size and grain of the paper you have chosen. Leave an inch or so (a few extra centimeters) on the head and tail above the desired final height. Make a clean cut in the paper, then carefully measure page widths

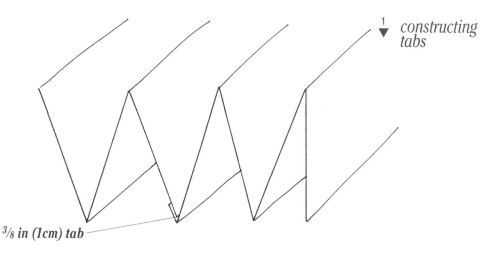

1 *constructing tabs*

3/8 in (1cm) tab

from that cut, marking each width with two pencil marks. On the last "page" of folded paper in the middle of the book, leave an extra ⅜ in (1cm) for the tab to connect it with the next series. Before folding into the accordion form, run over the width-marks with a folder (see the covering of glued books, page 26). The folds must be parallel. Assemble all the elements of the accordion: glue each tab with PVA and slip it over the first page of the next section. Secure the adhesion of the tab with the flat part of a folder. Check to make sure no glue has seeped out to stick pages together, and then let dry under weights. Trim the head and tail edges (see Pierced and sewn books, page 53).

THE COVER. The cover consists of two hard cover boards and two pieces of card, all of the same size. The squares should be around 1/16 in (2mm). The height and width should be those of the pages, plus the two squares. Cut the four pieces of the cover (see page 21).

• **The picture window.** On one of the two cover boards, determine the position of the image to be framed within the picture window. Make guide marks with a compass and draw the boundaries of the picture window. Then open the window, beginning each cut a fraction of an inch (1mm) beyond the corners, so that they will be clean and neat. Save the piece you cut out. Sand the cover board and the edges of the window. Glue one of the pieces of manila card onto the second cover board. Press, then let dry under weights. Sand the second cover board.

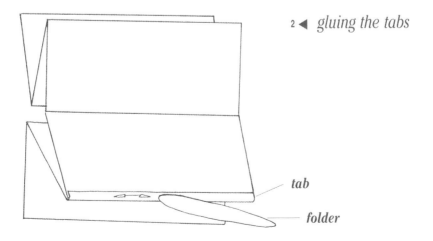

2 ◀ *gluing the tabs*

tab

folder

accordion books

• *Covering the outside of the covers.* First, determine the size of the paper to cover the boards and the manila card. Allow for 9/16 in (1.5cm) turn-ins on all sides. Cut and cover (see Covering the inside of the cover, Pierced and tied books, page 42). Cut away the fabric covering the picture window of the recto cover board: place the knife against each of the corners and a corner square against the knife, then cut at a 45-degree angle. Glue the turn-ins to the cover board. Let dry, then trim the turn-ins to 5/16 in (8mm). Place the image face down on the picture window so that it is properly framed; mark its position, then glue it in place. Press and let dry. Glue the manila card to the verso of the recto cover board and let dry, first in the press and then under weights.

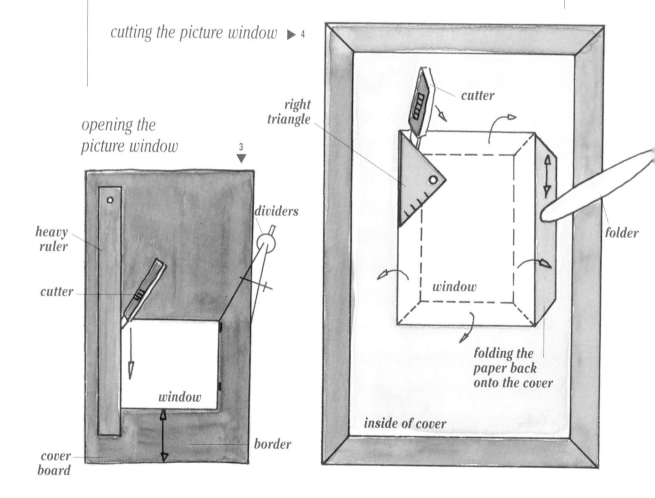

cutting the picture window ▶ 4

opening the picture window 3 ▼

right triangle

cutter

heavy ruler

dividers

folder

cutter

window

folding the paper back onto the cover

window

border

inside of cover

cover board

ASSEMBLING THE BOOK. Place the verso cover board face down on the work surface, with the pages of the book on top, leaving the proper squares all around. Without moving the stack, slide a piece of waste paper beneath the first (top) page, and apply glue. Carefully remove the waste paper. Brace two footed squares against the edges of the verso cover board, on the head and fore-edges. Slip the recto cover down along the squares onto the glued first page. Press down lightly and then lift the board to check adhesion. After protecting the cover image with the scrap of board removed from the window, slide a sheet of plastic beneath the first page, and press for a few minutes. Glue the verso cover board in the same fashion: glue the last page, and guide your placement of the board with the squares against the recto board. Press for a few minutes, and then let dry completely under weights.

sewn books

*A*nother soft-covered variation for notebook lovers, to be kept in a handbag or pocket, ready for whenever the time comes to write.

Preparation

MATERIALS. Sheets of paper for the pages and colored endpapers; PVA and wheat-flour paste; linen thread or other strong thread; two small strips of ribbon or other material (for the "beggar's pouch"); 10-point manila card, covered with paper, fabric, or thin leather, or thick reprocessed leather or thick wrapping paper; material to line the inside of the "beggar's pouch," and leather for its case; ornaments and clasp; sheets of plastic, waste paper, and card to protect your work; ribbon for the bookmark.

THE MODEL. These books are constructed from one or several sewn signatures; the pages are sewn into a one-piece soft cover. The sewing can be concealed or visible on the spine. The "beggar's pouch" can be refilled with fresh signatures, using the same cover, so it should be constructed from durable materials.

Sewing a single signature

THE PAGES. Fold and cut sheets of paper for the pages of the book (and colored endpapers, if desired). Assemble the sheets to form a single signature, and tap. Press the signature (see Pierced and tied books, page 36).

PERFORATIONS. To pierce the spine of the signature, first make a paper template, of the same height as the signature and 2⅜ in (6cm) wide. Fold it in half three times along the longer axis (for a total of seven folds), then fold twice along the shorter axis. Ease the template along the interior of the signature's spine-edge, and hold it in place

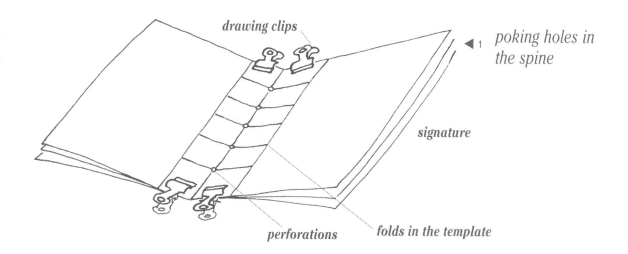

drawing clips

◀ 1 *poking holes in the spine*

signature

perforations *folds in the template*

with drawing clips. With an awl, pierce an odd number of evenly spaced holes in the spine, following the folds of the template. The number of folds depends on the height of the signature. Remove the template.

SEWING THE SIGNATURE. Thread a needle with a length of linen thread four times the height of the signature. Run the needle through the middle hole, from the outside to the inside of the spine, leaving half the thread on either side. Run the thread through one of the next holes and continue sewing a running stitch to the furthest hole (See Japanese-style sewn books, page 63). Then sew back to the middle hole. Leave that thread in the middle, and thread the needle with the other half of the thread. Run the needle through the next hole (from outside to inside), and proceed as for the first half. Knot the two ends of the thread on the inside of the spine with a flat knot.

TRIMMING THE EDGES. These cuts must run exactly parallel the opposite edges. First, trim the fore-edge. Place a footed square against the spine of the signature. Place a ruler against the square and mark the desired width in two places on the first page. Place the signature on a cutting board and a heavy ruler over the guide marks. Then, cut the pages with a well-sharpened cutting tool, in as many passes as necessary. In like fashion, proceed to trim the remaining edges.

Book edges were originally cut with a knife blade or scissors. The appearance of gilded edges, however, required that the edges be perfectly smooth; thus, in the sixteenth century, bookbinders took to using a plow (see page 54, figure 3). These continued to be used until the invention of the paper guillotine around 1850. The plow is still used by binders who prefer its characteristic edges. In this case, the goal is to cut all the pages of a sewn signature cleanly; this technique is close to those of professional bookbinding.

2 ▼   *pattern of sewing . . .*

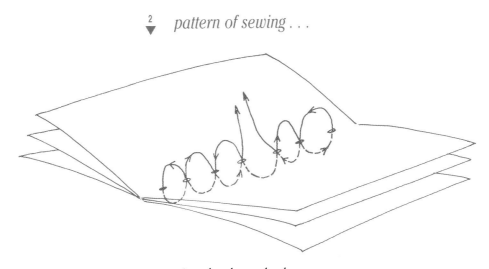

pierced and sewn books

THE BOOKMARK AND HEADBANDS. The ribbon for the bookmark should be about 1½ in (4cm) longer than the diagonal of the signature. Glue it to the spine with PVA, with ⅜ in (1cm) folded over the back. The rest of its length hangs into the interior of the signature.

Bookmarks were used to mark the pages of religious texts in the Middle Ages. Less common today, the thin ribbon of colored silk allows you to mark or easily find a given page in a book.

The headbands are constructed in the same way as for glued books (see page 29).

THE COVER, CLOSURE, AND CASE. See Glued books, starting on page 26, particularly the section on chemises, for construction of chemises with one or two flaps. When making a chemise for a book with only a single signature, it is not necessary to crease the spine of the jacket with a folder. If you want the stitching to be visible, you can sew the cover along with the signature. The order of construction would then be: cutting of pages, piercing, constructing bookmark and headbands, making cover and covering, sewing, closure, and decoration.

Sewing multiple signatures

THE PAGES. Fold and cut sheets of papers for the signatures; if desired, add colored endpapers. Tap and press the signatures.

PERFORATIONS. Follow the directions for piercing single signatures, but now make an even number of holes.

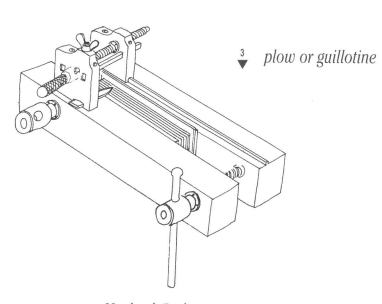

3 ▼ *plow or guillotine*

SEWING. The signatures are sewn together in sets of two adjacent holes. For each set of holes, thread a needle at one end of a medium-weight linen thread; the length of the thread should be the distance between the two holes times the number of signatures, plus 8in (20cm) for easier handling. Run the needle through the most right-hand hole of the top signature, from the outside to the inside of the spine, and then back out through the adjacent hole. Thread another needle at the tail end of the thread (on the right side). Run the second needle through the most right-hand hole of the second signature, again from the outside to the inside, and then again back out through the next hole. Then run the first needle (on the left hole of the first signature) through the same hole (the left hole of the second signature), and back out the adjacent right hole. The threads cross inside the second signature, bringing together the first two signatures at the first set of holes. Sew the third and subsequent signatures in the same way, and then sew the other sets of holes. Make sure the thread of each series is taut, so that the stitchwork is tight. Tie the thread of the first set of holes at the last signature. Thread a needle with the thread of the right hole and wind around the sewing thread between each signature. Then thread it through the right hole of the first signature, from outside to inside, and then from inside to outside through the left hole. Do the same (in reverse) with the slack thread of the left hole, then tie the two threads together with a double knot. Tie the other threads in the same way and trim any excess.

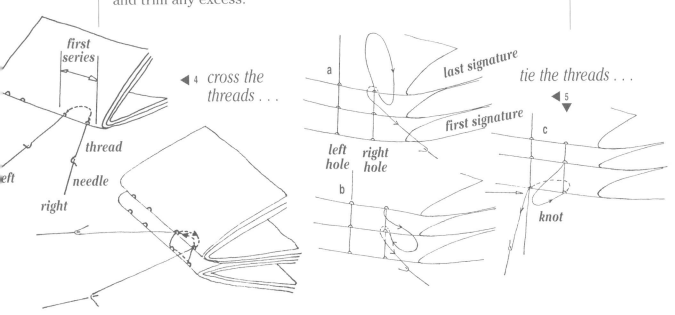

cross the threads . . .

tie the threads . . .

pierced and sewn books

55

GLUING. See Glued books, starting page 26. Trim the head, tail, and fore-edge, and add headbands and bookmark if desired.

COVER, CLOSURE, AND CASE. See "Glued books." Crease the cover with a folder, and then cover it. Make a closure if desired, and then assemble the book block and cover. Finish by decorating the cover.

Sewing multiple signatures with visible stitching

THE PAGES. Fold and cut sheets to make five or six signatures. Tap, press, and trim.

PERFORATIONS. Follow the directions on page 52, but now make an even number of holes. There should be at least as many holes in each signature as there are signatures in the book.

COVER AND CLOSURE. Make a cover from card (see Glued books). Crease the spine with a folder. Transfer the location of the holes onto the inside of the spine: with dividers, precisely mark the properly spaced placement of each of the holes in between each signature. Pierce the holes with an awl (see Glued books). Cover the card, and carefully pierce it again with a fine needle at the holes. You can add a closure, if desired.

6 ▼

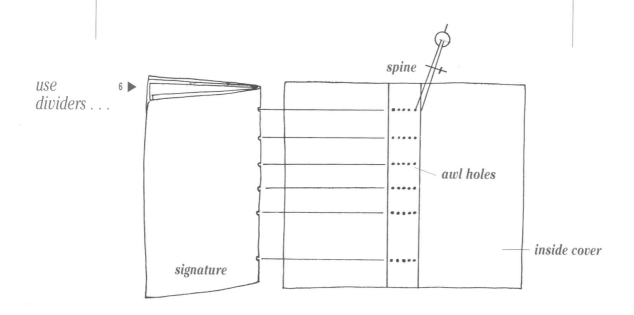

use dividers . . . 6 ▶

spine

awl holes

inside cover

signature

SEWING. Thread a needle with a length of thread six or seven times the height of the book. The stitching goes from signature to signature, along the height of the book. Start by sewing a running stitch from the top to the bottom signature, from the first row of holes on the right side of the cover. Run the thread from the outside to the inside. At the last hole, connect with the next signature. Sew all the signatures the same way, making sure to keep the threads taut. Run the head and tail of the thread through the facing holes on the inside of the book and knot them. Cut the excess thread. Finish by decorating the book.

The "beggar's pouch" book

The "beggar's pouch" book is small, but refillable. The sketchbook is a larger version of the beggar's pouch, constructed in the same way, but without a case.

THE PAGES. Fold and cut sheets for two small signatures, for example, $2\frac{1}{4}$ x 5in (6 x 13cm). You can make additional signatures in advance to refill the pouch. Trim the signatures.

PERFORATIONS. See Pierced and sewn books, page 52. Perforate each signature four times, at the second, third, fifth, and sixth folds of the template.

In the fifteenth century, travelers would commonly carry with them a little book called a "beggars pouch" book on their belt. Wherever they went, they carried it with them, protected in a case, held on their belt. Assuming they had a writing implement, they would be always prepared.

pierced and sewn books

THE COVER. Construct the cover from 10-point card, following the directions for glued books. Crease the spine with a folder. If you plan to cover it with thin leather, use wheat-paste on the leather, let dry overnight under weights, and trim the turn-ins. Cut two small pieces of tape, 1in (2.5cm) high, and 1½ in (4cm) wider than the spine (¾ in [2cm] for each side, to be glued to the verso). Carefully transfer the location of the holes in the signatures to the tapes, and perforate each tape twice for each set of holes in the signatures. Cut four 10in (25cm) lengths of stout linen thread, and run two pieces through each tape, perpendicular to the spine, so that an equal amount of thread extends over each end. **Position the signatures inside the open cover, leaving the proper squares all around. Hold firmly. Slide the tapes in place beneath the signatures, and align the holes in the cover with the perforations of the signatures. Mark the placement of the tapes, and glue them to the inside of the cover with PVA.**

7 ▼

7 ▼ *cut two small pieces of tape . . .*

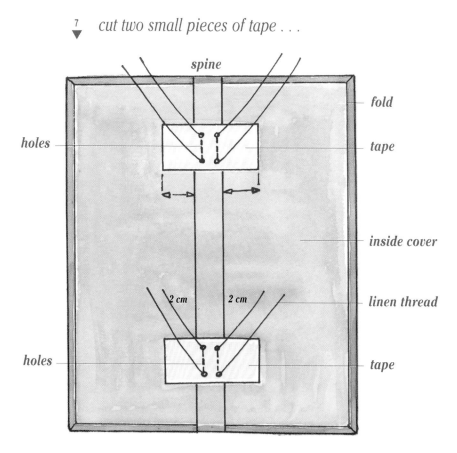

• *Covering the inside of the cover.* Use a strong and flexible material: suede lining, synthetic suede, imitation leather (sold in bookbinding supply stores), linen, or paper. Determine the proper dimensions of the covering materials as follows:

— the width should be that of the cover less twice ⅛ in (3mm).

— the height should be that of the cover less twice ⅛ in (3mm).

Cut, check the size, and trim if necessary. Poke holes in the covering material for the threads to run through. Apply glue to half the material and affix it to the cover, leaving the proper space for squares. Run the threads through the holes in the material, glue, and affix the other half. Press and then let dry completely under weights. Thread a needle with the loose threads from the cover, run them into the inside of the corresponding signature, and knot.

THE CASE FOR THE "BEGGAR'S POUCH" BOOK. First, determine the dimensions of the leather skin needed for the case. The width should be the height of the book plus ¾ in (2cm). The height should be twice the width of the book, plus the width of the flap.

Cut the leather and fold into the shape of the case. With an awl or needle, make a series of perforations along each side, ⅛ in (3mm) from the edge and ⅛ in (3mm) apart from one another. Mark the location of the loops on the back of the pouch, and poke holes ⅛ in (3mm) from the top and bottom of each. Stitch the loops and then the pouch with linen thread, and construct the clasp mechanism.

constructing the case

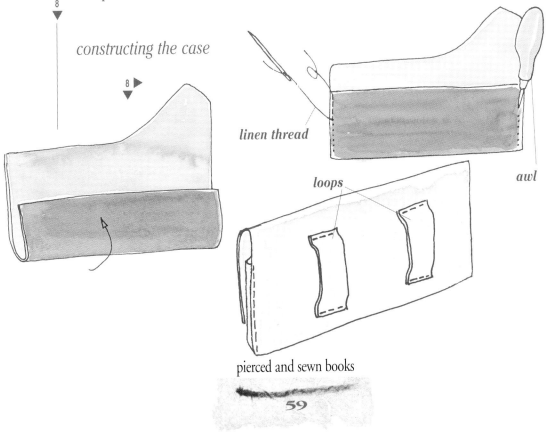

linen thread

loops

awl

pierced and sewn books

sewn books

Subtle, with only a bare whisper of the exotic, these books let the beautiful papers within play the starring role. Paper lovers will find them irresistible.

Preparation

MATERIALS. Japanese, Indian, or hand-made papers for the pages; colored silk thread or cord; sturdy paper, leather, or lightweight board (to be covered) for the cover (optional).

THE MODEL. Japanese-style sewn books can be sewn with silk thread and left without a cover, or sewn with a soft cover, with or without a spine. The most important thing in stitching is to check the tautness of the thread after each stitch. For books with stiffer covers, make larger holes and sew with cord (as with Pierced and sewn books, page 52). You can also devise your own ways to sew your books. . . .

Construction

PAGES. Fold and cut sheets for the pages, without trimming the uneven edges. Proceed in the same fashion as for pierced and sewn books, but without pressing the pages (in order not to crush the paper fibers).

THE COVER. You can add a one-piece soft cover, which should be stronger than the pages of the book. First, determine the necessary dimensions. The width should be twice that of the pages plus the thickness of the spine plus two small squares (if desired). The height should be that of the pages plus two squares. For a cover without a spine, the two boards should be the same size as the pages, plus squares. Cut the cover.

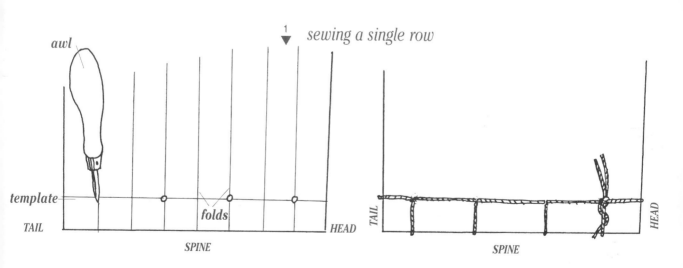

awl

template

TAIL

folds

SPINE

HEAD

1 ▼ *sewing a single row*

TAIL

SPINE

HEAD

Handmade Books

PERFORATIONS. The book should be pierced (with an awl or needle) about ¾ in (2cm) away from the spine edge (depending on the size of the book), using a template for proper positioning of the holes. The template should be of the same height as the spine, and 1½ in (4cm) wide. Fold it in half three times, place it along the spine, and clip it in place. Carefully mark the placement of the holes, which will be determined by the method you choose for sewing. Place the book on the striking block, make the holes, and remove the template.

SEWING.

• *Sewing a single row of holes.* Fold the template three times, unfold it and lay over the book, then pierce every other fold; remove the template. Thread a needle with a length of thread seven times the height of the book. Run the needle through the first hole nearest the head of the book, from the back to the front side. Wrap around the head of the book, sew a running stitch to the last hole (running stitch is sewn by running the needle through the hole before the last hole stitched), and wrap around the tail. Return toward the head, wrapping around the spine at each hole. Tie the two ends of the thread with a flat double knot under the first page, and cut off the excess thread.

• *Sewing a double row of holes.* Fold the template three times, unfold it and lay over the book, then make two rows of staggered holes. Pierce every other fold for the first row, and pierce holes in between for the second row. Remove the template. Thread a needle with a length of thread seven times the height of the book plus 12in

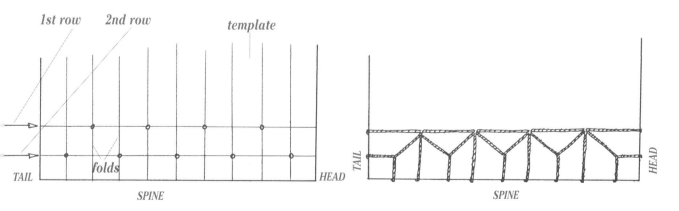

2 ▼ *sewing a double row*

1st row   2nd row   template

TAIL   HEAD   TAIL   HEAD

SPINE   SPINE

folds

Japanese-style sewn books

(30cm). Run the needle though the first hole of the first row nearest the head of the book, from the back to the front side, and wrap the thread around the head of the book. Continue with a running stitch to the tail edge of the first row. Return to the head, now sewing together the holes of the two rows (some of the stitchwork will thus form a diagonal pattern). Wrap the thread around the head edge at the second row of holes, and then around the spine, running it through each of the holes of both rows (making the second diagonal of the triangle pattern of stitches connecting the two rows). Wrap the thread around the tail edge of the second row, then return it to the head on the first row with a running stitch. Tie the two ends of the thread together with a flat knot under the first page. Cut off the excess thread.

• **_Sewing a double row of holes (variation)._** Fold the template three times and make two rows of holes:

— First row: pierce every fold

— Second row: pierce a hole $^3/_{16}$ in (5mm) on both sides of each fold. Remove the template. Thread a needle with fourteen times the height of the book plus 12in (30cm). Run a needle from the back to the front, through the first hole of the first row nearest the head of the book.

3
▼

Sewing a double row of holes (variation)

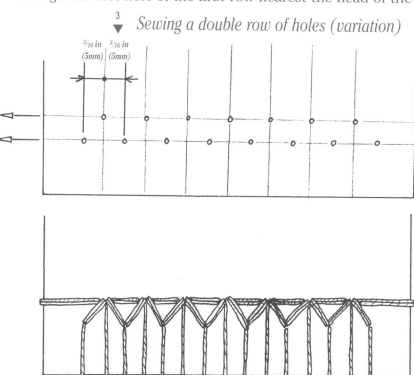

Sew a running stitch to the last hole of that row, then wrap the thread around the tail. Return to the head by sewing the rows together in sets of three holes, for a triangle pattern. To go from one set to the next, sew a running stitch on the first row of holes. Wrap the thread around the head edge. To get back to the tail, wrap the thread around the spine as you stitch each of the holes of the first row, doubling the stitch. Go from one hole to another with a running stitch on the first row; wrap around the tail. On the way back to the head, wrap around the spine as you stitch each of the holes of the second row, doubling the stitch. Go from one set of holes to the next by sewing a running stitch on the first row, and wrap around the head. Tie the two ends of the thread with a flat double knot under the first page, and cut the excess thread.

sunken cords

*F*ully cased
or with
laced-in
board covers,
these sturdy
notebooks
might hold
gourmet
recipes or
notes, serve
as log books
or guest
books . . .

Preparation

THE MATERIALS. Sheets of paper for the pages and colored end-papers; linen thread; linen or cotton tape, hemp twine, or strips of leather; PVA and wheat-flour paste; muslin or other lightweight fabric; colored ink and a cake of beeswax for decorating the edges; ribbon for a bookmark (optional); paper to line the spine; 10- or 12-point manila card for a soft cover and flapless chemise, or $\frac{1}{16}$ in (2mm) gray cardboard for a hard cover; paper or fabric for covering covers and chemise; decorative elements and closure; waste paper, sheets of plastic and card to protect your work.

THE MODEL. There are two types of sewn book with sunken cords. The first is cased in (that is, it has a case). Prepare the book up to the point of covering it. You then have the choice of a one-piece soft cover, as for glued books, or a hard cover. The hard-covered sewn binding is laced-in (with sewing cords passing through the boards) like traditional fine binding. This needs careful sewing, since the spine is covered with leather or fabric.

Sewn cased-in books with sunken cords

THE PAGES. Fold and cut paper for the pages and one or two signatures of colored endpapers. Tap and press.

SAWING. The placement of the sunken cord stations is important. Determine their location by evenly dividing the space between two end-point stations. The position of these points, called the link stitch, is calculated using the squares as a unit of measure. The head point should be at a distance of two squares from the head; the tail point, four squares from the tail (when measuring these figures, take the planned trimming of the pages into account). The number of cords or tapes depends on the size and shape of the book and the type of binding desired. The placement of the stations is marked with the help of a template with guide marks. For the linen thread you can substitute linen or leather strips, or hemp twine with strands separated. You then make shallow slots that do not penetrate very far into the spine but are just deep enough for the sewing thread. The stitching thus holds

In the sixteenth century, bookbinders imported from Italy a new technique of sewing, consisting of lodging leather bands in slots that were sawed in the spine. This method is called sewing with sunken cords. At first forbidden, it was later tolerated for common binding, and authorized after 1700 for ordinary binding. The technique is commonly practiced today in ordinary binding, the slots now housing hemp twine. At each end of the spine, two extra slots, called link stitches, have been added, through which to run the thread from one signature to another.

the back less firmly than when the cord is placed deeper inside the spine, but the book opens more easily. Determine the amount of paper that will be trimmed from the pages—from ¾ in to 2 in (2cm to 5cm), depending on the size of the book. Mark the spaces that will be trimmed from the book on the spines of the signatures, and mark the head and tail link-stitch stations two and four squares, respectively, from the planned trim edges. Divide the distance between the link-stitch stations into six equal sections, with five guide marks. (Depending on the size of the book, you can make between two and five slots.) Distribute the cuts evenly, so that the spine will hold together properly. For sewing with tape (or separated twine), the guide marks for the slots represent the center of the tape (or cord). Make the cuts on both sides of the guide marks, half as far away from the mark as the width of the tape (or cord). Place two wedges of ⅛ in (3mm) cardboard under the edges of the press to lift it a little so the spine of the book will be out of the press a fraction of an inch. Open the press and slide in the signatures, fore-edges facing you, spines resting on the work surface. Square the head side of the signatures. Close the press tightly. Turn the press up. Place one side of the press on the work surface and the other side on the back of a chair or other horizontal surface at the same height. Access to the fore-edge should not be blocked by any surface beneath. Extend the guide marks down the width of the spine, and cut the slots evenly with a small metal saw, cutter, or scalpel held at right angles to the spine. The cuts must all be of the same depth and must not go past the sheet of the central signature.

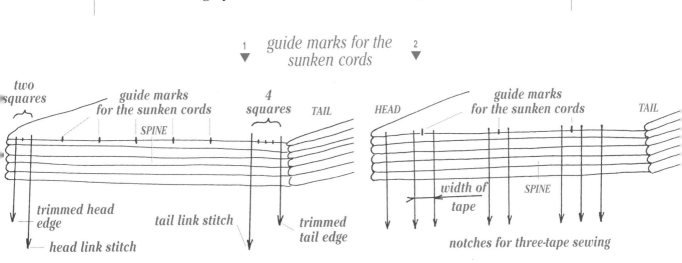

1 ▼ *guide marks for the sunken cords* 2 ▼

two squares

guide marks for the sunken cords

4 squares TAIL

HEAD

guide marks for the sunken cords

TAIL

SPINE

trimmed head edge

tail link stitch

trimmed tail edge

width of tape

SPINE

head link stitch

notches for three-tape sewing

sewn books with sunken cords

SEWING ON A SEWING FRAME. Sewing frames are available at binding supply stores, but with only a little work you can also construct a serviceable and inexpensive frame yourself. 3 ▼

Eleventh-century bookbinding monks were the first to use sewing frames. At that time, the frames were fixed: that is, composed of two pieces of wood and two threaded risers on which the threads or tapes were stretched.

After sewing, depending on the type of binding and thread, the spine will be around a third larger. The choice of thread size is very important. It depends on three factors: the type of paper used; the thickness of the signatures; and the number of signatures. For softer papers, the thread should be half the thickness of a signature. For harder papers, it should be one-third the thickness of a signature. Thus, if a paper is hard, but your book has many thin signatures, the thread should be thin. If the paper is soft and your book has only a few thick signatures, the thread must be stout. The choice of thread is easier when you are constructing a new book from new paper than when you are sewing an old book. Place the first signature on the bottom board of the sewing frame, the head on the right side, tapes placed over their corresponding slots. Thread a long blunt-tipped needle with about 36 in (1m) of thread. Run the needle through the head link-stitch station, from the outside to the inside of the first signature. Bring the needle through the first slot, go over the tape, and re-enter the spine through the second slot. Go over the other tapes in the same way. Run the needle through the tail link-stitch station to go from the inside to the outside of the first signature's spine. Place the second signature on top of the first, lining up the

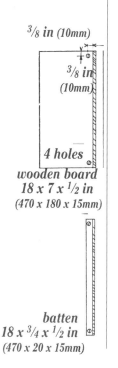

³⁄₈ in (10mm)

³⁄₈ in (10mm)

4 holes

wooden board
18 x 7 x ¹⁄₂ in
(470 x 180 x 15mm)

batten
18 x ³⁄₄ x ¹⁄₂ in
(470 x 20 x 15mm)

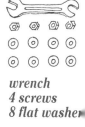

wrench
4 screws
8 flat washers

▶ 4

4 wood feet

two threaded rods
3³⁄₄ in (98mm) diameter, 8 in (210mm) long

two steel tubes
³⁄₈ x ¹⁄₂ in (10 x 12mm)
6¹⁄₄ in (160mm) long

3 ▼ *constructing the sewing frame*

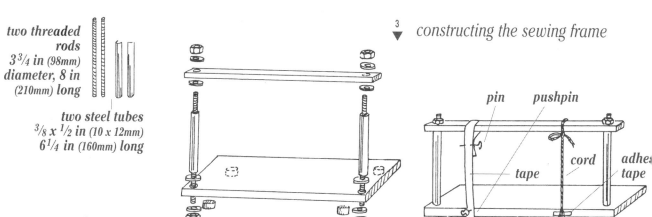

pin   pushpin

cord   adhes tape

tape

head edges. Run the needle from the outside to the inside of the second signature through the tail link stitch. Sew over the tapes as with the first signature, and end by running the needle from the inside to the outside of the second signature at the head link stitch. Make sure the threads are properly taut, pulling the threads along the spine, so as not to tear the paper. Check that the two signatures are aligned at the head and close together along the spine. Knot the two threads with a double knot, then lodge the knot inside the slot. Place the third signature on the frame, sew its spine, and attach it to the second signature at the link-stitch station: run the needle between the first two signatures to the right of the tail station and bring it out on the left side behind the thread; pull the thread taut in the link-stitch station. Sew the other signatures in the same way. Make sure that the stitching is tight after sewing each signature. When you have sewn all of them, make a double knot and cut off the excess thread. Remove the tapes from the sewing frame. To tie two threads together, make a weaver's knot and, if possible, lodge it within a slot or within a signature. The weaver's knot is tied by running a length of a second thread through a loop at the end of the first thread, then looping the second thread around the loop. Pull on the four strands to tighten the knot, then trim off the shorter ends.

GLUING. Tap the sewn book well on the spine and head. Pull on the tapes to make sure that they are tight on the spine. Check that all the signatures are well secured at the spine. With the thumb and forefinger of your left hand, hold the book on the work surface. Glue

5 ▼

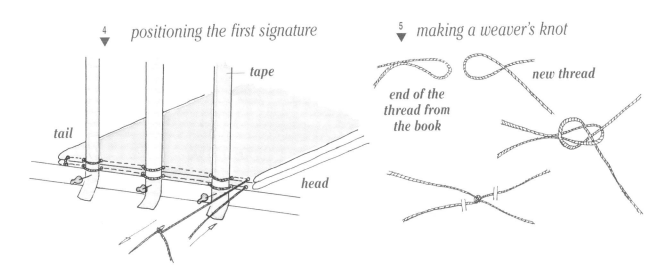

4 ▼ *positioning the first signature*

tape

tail

head

5 ▼ *making a weaver's knot*

new thread

end of the
thread from
the book

sewn books with sunken cords

the spine with PVA, from the middle toward the head and then toward the tail, so as not to get glue on the edges. Rub the spine with the edge of a hammer so the glue spreads between the signatures. Tap the glued spine on a piece of waste paper. Square the spine and head of the book, and let dry under weights. Cut the tapes down to ¾ in (2cm) longer than the width of the spine on either end, and glue the excess to the first and last sheet (or the endpapers).

APPLYING THE MUSLIN. The fabric strengthens the spine of the book. Put the book in a press, with the spine as close as possible to the upper edge. Apply the fabric in the same fashion as with glued books.

TRIMMING. Trim the head and tail edges following the guide marks made earlier; then trim the fore-edge (see Pierced and sewn books, page 50).

DECORATING THE EDGES. Color the head edge of the book as follows. First, place the well-squared and securely bound book in the press, the head toward you and protruding a fraction of an inch (1mm). Close the press very tightly, making sure the jaws remain parallel. Set up the press in the same way as for sawing slots. Sand the edge of the book with medium-grit sandpaper, following the direction of the pages (from spine to fore-edge). Clear away the dust as you go with a brush. Sand again with very fine sandpaper, taking care not to press so hard that you score the surface. After sanding, the edge should be mirror-smooth. Apply wheat-flour paste to the edge, wipe off the excess paste, and run over the edge a cotton ball soaked in ink and squeezed dry. Let the book dry in the press. You can wax the edge using the inner side of a piece of leather rubbed in a cake of beeswax. If you have an agate burnisher, you can also polish the edge. Add bookmark and headbands, if desired.

Decorated and colored edges became popular in the Middle Ages. After the sixteenth century, the smooth edges of books trimmed with a plow made gilding feasible. The most ornate books of that time had edges chiseled and gilded, gilded on a marbled base, or gilded on a chiseled marbled base. In the nineteenth century, "Oriental" edges were marbled after gilding, or gilded and decorated with miniature designs. Since the beginning of the twentieth century, gilded edges have been applied to untrimmed books, only the longest (that is, protruding) sheets being gilded.

LINING THE SPINE WITH PAPER. Like muslin, paper is used to strengthen the spine and also to even out the differences in height across the spine caused by the tapes and headbands. Cut two strips of paper, of the same width as the spine. The first strip fills out the spine between the two headbands; its height should be that of the

▶ 6

spine less the combined height of the headbands. The second strip covers the whole spine, and thus is of the same height as the spine. Wet the two strips with a moist, wrung-out sponge. Glue the spine with PVA and apply the first strip. Rub over the strip, lightly covered with paste, using a bone folder to adhere it to the spine. Glue the covered spine with PVA and apply the second strip of paper. Let it dry in the press. Sand the spine diagonally with very fine sandpaper, applying pressure over the location of the tapes. The spine should be perfectly smooth after sanding. Now you can choose the type of cover: either a one-piece soft cover (constructed in the same way as for glued books) or a hard cover.

THE HARD COVER. First, determine the height of the cover boards, leaving squares on the head, tail, and fore-edge. The width of the boards should be that of the signatures plus one square. The height should be that of the signatures plus two squares. See Pierced and tied books (page 50) for cutting the cover. From the same board as the cover boards, cut a rectangle for the spine. Its height should be the same as that of the cover boards, its width that of the spine. Sand the three pieces of board.

• ***Covering the outside of the cover.*** The width of the covering material should be the two turn-ins plus twice the width of the cover boards plus the width of the spine plus twice the thickness of the board. Its height should be two turn-ins plus the height of the cover boards. Lay the material face down on the work surface. Place a heavy ruler above the bottom edge of the head turn-in. Position the first cover board along the ruler, leaving the proper space for the turn-ins, and mark its four corners. Position the spine board next to the first board, at a distance of one thickness of the

6 ▼ *determining the size of the paper strips*

▶ 7

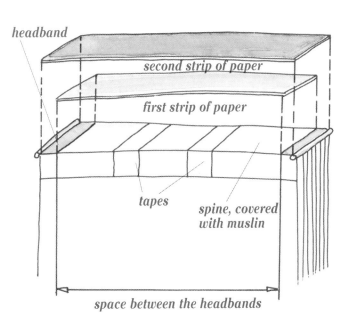

headband

second strip of paper

first strip of paper

tapes

spine, covered with muslin

space between the headbands

sewn books with sunken cords

board, and mark its corners. Finally, position the second cover board another thickness away from the spine board and mark its corners. To glue the cover, follow the same procedure as for covering the exterior of glued book covers. Place the book block within the cover, sliding sheets of plastic between the cover boards and endpapers. Press for a few minutes, then let dry completely under weights. See Glued books (page 24) for closure and casing in.

THE FLAPLESS CHEMISE. A chemise without flaps is constructed in similar fashion as the covers of glued books. First, determine the necessary dimensions of the manila card. Add a small square of $\frac{1}{16}$ in (2mm) to protect the book. The width should be twice that of the book plus the width of the spine plus two squares. The height should be that of the book plus two squares. Cut the chemise and crease the edges of the spine with a folder; finish the chemise following the directions for covering glued books.

• *Covering the outside of the chemise.* The width of the covering material should be the two turn-ins plus the total width of the jacket. The height should be the two turn-ins plus the height of the chemise. Cut and glue following the same method as for glued books. The chemise can include a closure, if desired.

position the heavy ruler . . .

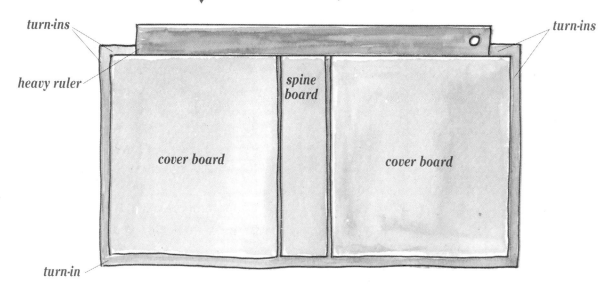

turn-ins   turn-ins

heavy ruler

spine board

cover board   cover board

turn-in

- ***Covering the inside of the chemise.*** First, determine the necessary dimensions of the material. The height should be the height of the chemise less twice ⅛ in (3mm). The width should be the width of the chemise less twice ⅛ in (3mm). For gluing, see covering the exterior of cover boards of pierced and tied books (page 43).

Sewn laced-in books with sunken cords

Prepare the signatures and colored endpapers; tap and press.

PREPARATION. Prepare the spine for sewing with untwisted hemp twine, the guide marks for the notches representing the middle of the cords. With an awl, separate the strands of 2 or 3in or so (5 to 8 cm) of the twine along the spine; remove the loose hairs as you go, but do not thin the strands too much.

SEWING. Attach the cord to the batten of the sewing frame and stick it to the board with adhesive tape. Sew the book by following the directions for sewing on the frame, page 70.

GLUING. Follow the directions on page 71, but do not cut the threads after gluing the spine. Trim the head, tail, and fore-edges with the plow or guillotine.

ROUNDING THE BACK. The rounding of the spine prepares it for the backing. The linen thread plays an important role here: if properly chosen, it will give a swell to the spine after sewing, making the following operations easier. Rounding the signatures with a hammer makes a curve in the spine of the book. Wait about half an hour after gluing, so the spine will still be flexible, and place the book flat on a hard surface. With the fore-edge facing you, hold it firmly in place with your left hand, fingers spread on top of the book block, thumb on the fore-edge. With your right hand, hold the hammer so as to strike with the flat side of the head. Start with the side of the spine resting on the work surface. Strike the signatures all along the length of the spine, from head to tail and then softly back to the top part. Lower the handle of the hammer to get an almost horizontal striking surface. Manipulate the angle of the book with your left hand. Turn the block over and strike again, starting with the middle signatures. Repeat until the spine is well curved.

BACKING. Shaping the spine requires a press with backing boards. If you do not have one, you can still construct a cover for your book

▶ 8

sewn books with sunken cords

after rounding the back without backing. Rounding the back was a first step toward backing, an operation that creates shoulders within which the cover boards are lodged. The size of the shoulders depends on the thickness of the board used for the cover. With dividers, measure the thickness of the board, then mark the distance on the spine sides of the front and back endpapers, at the head and tail. Place the book between the backing boards in the press (leave the tapes on the outside). Carefully adjust the jaws of the backing boards to align with the four marks made earlier, put in the press, and apply moderate pressure. Check the two endpapers at their heads and tails to be sure they extend past the jaws equally, and that the curve of the spine is even; the spine must be exactly parallel to the jaws of the boards. Close the press tightly. Hold the hammer by the head, between thumb and forefinger, and wrap your other fingers around the end of the handle. Pressing the rounded part of the hammer over the head and tail, shape the signatures into a fan pattern. Leave the central signatures as they are; they should remain straight. Start from the middle of each side, softly pulling the signatures toward the jaws of the press. This operation readies the signatures for backing. Then, strike slantwise toward the shoulders with ample motion on the signatures, following the curve of the spine so as to roll the signatures toward the jaws of the press. Start at one end and strike twenty or so times along the spine of the first signatures as you move toward the other end. Return to the starting point and strike over another row. Leave the signatures progressively

9 ▼

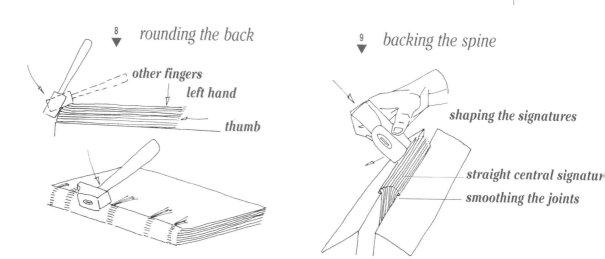

8 ▼ *rounding the back*

other fingers

left hand

thumb

9 ▼ *backing the spine*

shaping the signatures

straight central signatur

smoothing the joints

Handmade Books

more slanted toward the edges, and then, using the hammer, smooth the shoulders of the first signatures on either side all along the spine.

THE COVER BOARDS. See instructions for the hard cover on page 73, but only cut the two cover boards and not the spine piece. Cover the exterior of the boards.

• *Lacing-in.* In traditional binding, the cover is usually sewn on cords that are laced through the boards, while in case binding the cover is prepared separately and attached to the book block by the endpapers. You can borrow the former technique to construct your books. First, determine the location of the slits: they should be as wide as the cord you are using and cut ⅜ in (1cm) from the edge of the spine. Place the book block within the covers, leaving the proper space for squares, and lightly mark the location of the cords on the boards. Mark the location of a second set of slots about 1⅛ in (3cm) in front of the first ones (see illustration 8, page 76): the stitching will be visible on the cover, serving as a decorative element. Place the boards on a striking block and pierce the slits with a chisel. Wet the ends of the cords with PVA, keeping them flat. Run the cords through the first series of slits, from the inside to the outside of the cover boards, and then through the second series of slits. Open the cover board against the spine of the book. Pull on the cords to check that they are taut and that the book closes correctly. Place the open cover on the work surface, face down, and tap the slits closed with a hammer. Glue the ends of the cords in a fan pattern on the inside face of the cover board with PVA. Let dry with the board hanging open over the edge of the work surface. Proceed in the same way for the second cover board. Tap the glued cords with a hammer to flatten them, and tap along the spine to make the signatures flush with the cover.

• *Gluing the cords.* Glue the cords to the inside of the cover board. Hold the book with the spine toward you and check that the squares are even. Lift the front cover board, apply a little PVA to the threads with the folder, and close the book. Glue the cords to the verso, or inside of the board. Square the book. Let dry completely under weights. Cover the insides of the covers (see Pierced and tied books, page 39), and add a closure, if desired.

albums

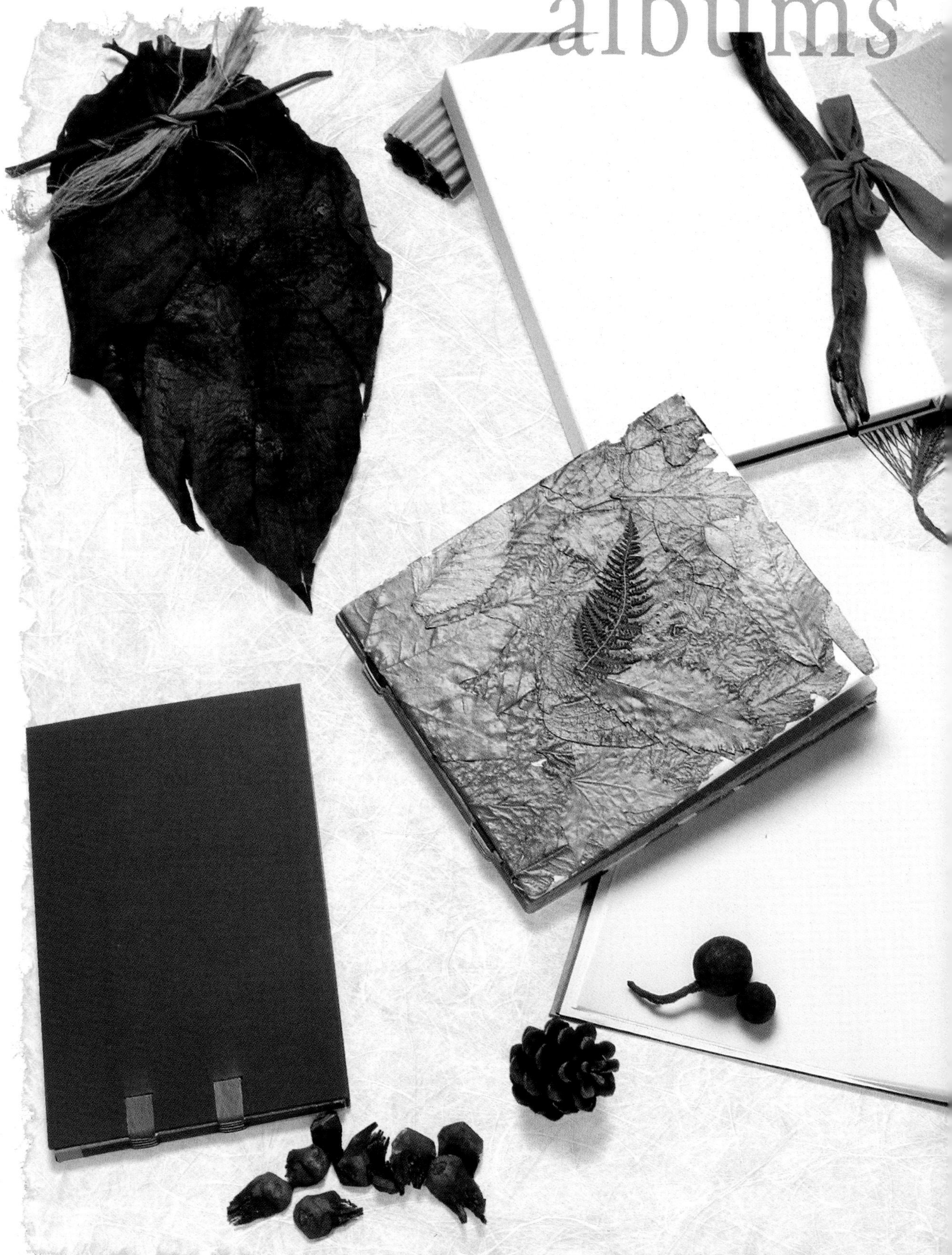

with guards

Albums for collecting pictures, flowers, potpourri, bric-à-brac, found objects: to forget nothing, to remember summer in the heart of winter.

Preparation

THE MATERIALS. Sheets of sturdy recycled paper or photo-album paper, for the pages; sheets of paper for colored endpapers; linen thread and tape or leather strips; PVA; $\frac{3}{32}$ in (2mm) gray cardboard for cover boards; paper or fabric for covering the boards; decorative elements and closure; waste paper, sheets of plastic, and manila card to protect your work.

THE MODEL. These albums are constructed with a 1¼ in (3cm) fold in the sheets for the guards. Use a medium-weight paper, of at least 100-pound (180gsm) weight.

Construction

THE PAGES. First, determine the size of the album. Add 1¼ in (3cm) for the guards. With dividers, mark each sheet 1¼ in (3cm) toward the interior of the spine side, with guide marks near the head and tail for the guards. Crease with a folder (see covering glued books). Fold the guards. Cut one or two sheets for colored endpapers, without guards. You can glue to the guards pieces of translucent paper of the same size as the unfolded sheets, in order to protect the articles you will hold in the book. Place the sheets on top of one another, the guards toward you. Stack them two by two, turning the second sheet and sliding it within the guard of the first to make signatures that can be sewn with sunken cords. Slide between the pages of the album, against the guard of each sheet, a sheet of paper of the same thickness as the pages, to make up for the difference in thickness (you can use scraps of paper here). Tap the album well, and press.

FROM SAWING TO DECORATING. For sawing and sewing, see sewing on tapes for Sewn books with sunken cords (page 70). For gluing, see Glued books (page 27). Then trim the book (see Pierced and tied books, page 38). The covering is made in the same way as for sewn books with sunken cords. You can add a closure (see Glued books, page 33) or a picture window (see Accordion books, page 47) before decorating as you wish.